METAPHYSICS AND THE DISUNITY OF SCIENTIFIC KNOWLEDGE

For my mother

Metaphysics and the Disunity of Scientific Knowledge

STEVE CLARKE
Department of History and Philosophy of Science
University of Melbourne
Victoria, Australia

Ashgate

Aldershot • Brookfield USA • Singapore • Sydney

Published by
Ashgate Publishing Ltd
Gower House
Croft Road
Aldershot
Hants GU11 3HR
England

Ashgate Publishing Company
Old Post Road
Brookfield
Vermont 05036
USA

British Library Cataloguing in Publication Data
Clarke, Steve
    Metaphysics and the disunity of scientific knowledge. -
    (Avebury series in philosophy)
    1.Science - Philosophy
    I. Title
    501

Library of Congress Catalog Card Number: 97-78320

ISBN 1 85972 538 4

Printed and bound by Athenaeum Press, Ltd.,
Gateshead, Tyne & Wear.

Contents

Acknowledgements

This book is a descendant of my doctoral thesis which was submitted at Monash University in late 1994. My primary intellectual debts are to John Bigelow and Philip Pettit, who jointly supervised my doctoral work, as well as to Stuart Barnum, who closely read the penultimate draft of the book and discussed many of the issues with me. Others who particularly deserve thanks for their contributions to the development of the ideas found here include Jeremy Aarons, Jo Asscher, the late David Brooks, Nancy Cartwright, Alan Chalmers, Alan Crooke, John Fox, Philip Kitcher, Cathy Legg, Sandy Mitchell, Robert Nola, Don Ross, Jacques Roussouw, Howard Sankey, Michael Smith, Paul Taylor, Neil Thomason, and Damian Verdnik. Thanks are also due to Rawbone Malong for his Sow Theffricun Innglissh copy editing (big pawn?).

My doctoral work was supported by an Australian Postgraduate Research Award. The transformation of a rambling thesis into a book was assisted by Monash University, which provided me with a 'writing-up' award; the University of Cape Town, which provided me with a relief lectureship for two months in 1996; and the University of Melbourne Department of History and Philosophy of Science, which provided me with a visiting fellowship over the southern summer of 1996-7 when much of the reworking of the thesis took place.

The work draws upon two previously published papers. Section 2.3 is based on a paper published in the *Australasian Journal of Philosophy*. Section 3.5 is based on a paper published in *International Studies in the Philosophy of Science*. Full references are included in the bibliography. Thanks to Robert Young of the *Australasian Journal* and to Carfax International for permission to use the material.

Cape Town,
November 1997

Preface

The primary concern of this book is to show how a metaphysics can be developed, constrained by empiricist concerns for experience, mediated by the senses, which allows us to make sense of our situation as knowers who must *make do* in a world of uncertainty. We make do by learning to export and re-use knowledge obtained where we can get it, to other very different situations where worldly knowledge would otherwise elude us. Recently, a number of philosophers of science, notably Nancy Cartwright and John Dupré, have argued similarly, arguing for the possibility that we might be living in a metaphysically disorderly world in which a disunified account of science is appropriate.

In this book I support the case for treating the possibility of metaphysical disorder seriously, not by adding to the studies of science carried out by Cartwright, Dupré and others, which point to the reality of disunity amongst the sciences, but by showing how the ideas of contemporary disunifiers can be located in a broader philosophical context, and related to the history of modern western philosophy. It is hoped that this effort will make those ideas more accessible to philosophers and others who have not digested as much of the burgeoning science studies literature as would otherwise be required to appreciate the philosophical significance of the aforementioned authors.

While the concern to oppose unificationist views of science may seem like an exclusively late twentieth century preoccupation, I argue that it needs to be understood in the context of the perceived threat of metaphysical disorder that is a major concern throughout the course of modern philosophy. Indeed, the central current of ideas in modern philosophy — through Hume, Kant and Hegel, to the present — can be understood as a reaction to this threat. Embracing the possibility of metaphysical disorder enables the development of a pragmatic alternative to the scepticism that is implicit in much of contemporary postmodernism.

The need for a prag-matic alternative to contemporary postmodernism is made clear in Chapter One, which substantially consists in an attack on Rorty's sceptical post-modernist account of the history of modern philosophy. In the second chapter the ideas of Nancy Cartwright are introduced in context, and it is suggested that the appeal of postmodern scepticism may have to do with its superficial resemblance to a legitimate target which postmodernists intuitively sense, but fail to recognise clearly. This legitimate target is *fundamentalism* and Cartwright's opposition to it is explained as the concept of fundamentalism is explicated.

In Chapter Three several possible antifundamentalist philosophies are considered and found to be unsatisfactory. Groundwork for an antifundamentalist philosophy is the theme of Chapters Four and Five where the topics of causation and idealization are considered. The treatment of both of these topics is brought together to yield an outline of an antifundamentalist philosophy of science. In the final chapter the topic of unification of knowledge is returned to and it is shown that, surprisingly, the alternative to postmodern scepticism that I advocate has much in common with the views of Otto Neurath.

... throw metaphysics into the fire, and science goes with it, preserve science from the flames and metaphysics comes creeping back

John Passmore, *A Hundred Years of Philosophy*, p. 392.

1 Epistemology, Scepticism and Postmodernity

1.1 A wrong turn in Königsberg

The issues which will be discussed in this book have a lineage that traces back to some of the most central concerns in modern western philosophy. Consideration of that most classical family of problems in philosophy, the problems raised by the possibility of global scepticism, will serve as an entry point to the broader concerns to be addressed.

The global sceptic challenges us to provide a general justification for our knowledge claims, and there are three different sorts of ways in which we can react to this challenge. The first sort of reaction is to attempt to meet the sceptical challenge head-on; to accept the challenge and try to defeat the sceptic. A second is to acquiesce in the face of the challenge. A third reaction is to refuse to play the game on the sceptic's terms, but attempt instead to defend knowledge claims in a less than absolute way. This work is an argument of the third sort.

The depth of the challenge which the sceptic presents us with is captured by David Hume in his *Treatise of Human Nature*. The *Treatise* is a brilliant work and a repository of sceptical problems, the force of which was never as clearly and persuasively stated before Hume's time. Thomas Reid sums up the response subsequent philosophers have typically felt after making acquaintance with the *Treatise*:

> If [my mind] is indeed, what the *Treatise of Human Nature* makes it, I find I have been only in an enchanted castle, imposed upon by spectres and apparitions ... Des Cartes no sooner began to dig in this mine than scepticism was ready to break in upon him. He did what he could to shut it out. Malebranche and

1

Locke, who dug deeper, found the difficulty of keeping out this enemy still to increase; but they laboured honestly in the design. Then Berkeley, who carried on the work, despairing of securing all, bethought himself on an expedient: by giving up the material world, which he thought might be spared without loss, and even with advantage, he hoped by an impregnable partition to secure the world of spirits. But alas! the *Treatise of Human Nature* wantonly sapped the foundation of this partition, and drowned all in one universal deluge (Reid 1970, pp. 17-18).

Having alerted philosophers to the intractability of sceptical problems, Hume also recognised that the consequences of scepticism could be dramatically diminished by just one act of faith: faith in order. If we suppose that there is a determinate order out there in the world, waiting to be discovered, then we can avoid the host of sceptical problems raised by the possibility that the regularities we are able to observe might not be projectable, because the world might not be orderly.

How could things have been as they are, were there not an original, inherent principle of order somewhere, in thought or in matter? And it is very indifferent to which of these we give the preference. Chance has no place, on any hypothesis, sceptical or religious. Every thing is surely governed by steady, inviolable laws (Hume 1947, p. 174).

Hume's counsel in the face of the threat of disorder in the world seems to amount to the less-than-convincing advice that we simply pretend that that threat does not exist. However, in the suggestion that order might be found 'in thought', the passage hints at a subtler way in which the threat of underlying metaphysical disorder might be diffused. This suggestion is taken up by Kant, and motivates his transcendental idealism:

Thus the order and regularity in the appearances, which we entitle *nature*, we ourselves introduce. We could never find them in appearances, had not we ourselves, or the nature of our mind, originally set them there (Kant 1929, p. 147, A125).

Hume's and Kant's struggle against scepticism has been continued to this day by the majority of western philosophers, both analytic and European. In various ways philosophers since Hume and Kant attempt to defend us from the threat of global scepticism by presuming what I will call *fundamentalism*: the dogma that order, either discovered in or imposed on the world, is a fundamental condition of the possibility of knowledge about

2

the world. The term fundamentalism is one which I have adapted from Cartwright. It will be further discussed in Chapter Two.

Ultimately this defence against scepticism is doomed to failure. If we are to honestly count ourselves as thinkers who open-mindedly formulate our judgements about the world on the basis of empirical evidence, then we are not entitled to make presumptions about how that evidence will turn out. We are not entitled to the presumption that the world is substantially ordered in any particular way, and nor are we entitled to the presumption that the human mind is capable of imposing order on the world. Against the tradition of Hume and Kant we need to embrace the possibility of life in a disorderly world.

Kant's philosophy was powerfully influenced by Newton's physics (Friedman 1992b). In Kant's time it seemed that science had found the determinate order of the physical world. Today, in the wake of the demise of classical physics, we are much more cautious. Recently a small number of philosophers of science, principally Dupré and Cartwright, have begun to urge that we take seriously the possibility that this world is a disunified one, in which order is only sporadically found or created. It is time for the mainstream of philosophers to accept that a wrong turn was taken in Königsberg, and to take the possibility that we inhabit a disordered world seriously.

Because I hold that scientific knowledge is achievable despite the problem of disorder, my work can be seen as an alternative to contemporary postmodernisms, which currently dominate many of the humanities and the social sciences. Postmodernists rail against the 'Enlightenment' attitude of respect for scientific achievement. They see philosophy, particularly analytic philosophy, as attempting to provide the enlightenment with propaganda in the form of metaphysical and antimetaphysical schemas which privilege scientific knowledge. Postmodernists make much of the importance of sceptical concerns so as to drag scientific knowledge down to the level of its supposed alternatives.

Although I do not think that science is worthy of the slavish hero-worshipping that some recent philosophers have indulged in, I do think that scientific knowledge is epistemically superior to its competitors because it engages with the empirical world in a deeper way than those alternatives. I will go on to try to show how it does this in Chapters Four and Five. In the remainder of this chapter, I will further consider what is wrong with contemporary postmodernism, so as to diminish its appeal and to allow me to highlight the difference between it and the position that I advocate. I will focus my attention on one particular postmodernist,

Richard Rorty. Rorty is particularly influential, and, unlike other post-modernists, he has been critically engaged with contemporary analytic philosophy. Rorty does not explicitly describe himself as a postmodernist, claiming that the term postmodern is '... so over-used that it is causing more trouble than it is worth' (Rorty 1991, p. 1); however, his *Philosophy and the Mirror of Nature* (1980) is widely considered to be a postmodern work, and I will be in good company in treating it as one.

1.2 The death of epistemology?

Postmodern scepticism often appears in the guise of an attack on epistemology, the core discipline of modern philosophy. An influential body of opinion has it that nowadays we live in postmodern times and in these postmodern times there is no call for epistemology. This view is sometimes encapsulated in the catch-cry 'epistemology is dead'. Dead, because it is an intellectual activity which is conceptually bound to the past, and irrelevant to the present and the foreseeable future. On this view, the epistemology that is being done today is merely the vestigial trace of an intellectual discipline which appeared to be worth pursuing within the intellectual climate of our recent intellectual past. That recent past — the modern era — has been consigned to history, and the remnants of epistemology should now go the same way, or so an influential body of postmodern opinion informs us.

The Magnum Opus of the 'epistemology is dead' view is Richard Rorty's *Philosophy and the Mirror of Nature* (1980). Rorty's attack on epistemology, in (Rorty 1980), is part of a broader campaign against modern western philosophy, which is the intellectual tradition that epistemology has been predominantly practised in. Like other postmodern works, *Philosophy and the Mirror of Nature* has a historical focus, substantially consisting in an examination and rejection of the intellectual projects and ambitions of the modern era.

Against Rorty, I maintain that epistemology continues to be worth pursuing despite the demise of modernity. I'm going to argue for this conclusion in three ways. First, I will challenge Rorty's account of the place of epistemology within modern philosophy. I will argue that Rorty does not succeed in showing us that epistemology is tied sufficiently closely to modern philosophy to warrant the conclusion that the passing of modern philosophy also involves the death of epistemology. Second, I will critically examine and reject Rorty's characterisations of philosophy in the postmodern era as being free of epistemology. Finally, I will argue directly in favour of the conclusion that epistemology is an important activity now. I will argue that there are a variety of irreducibly epistemological practical concerns which continue to affect us in this postmodern age.

My lack of opposition to the claim that these are postmodern times is unlikely to endear me to many other opponents of Rorty, particularly those who associate the term *postmodernism* exclusively with this or that author or school which they also oppose. However, I do not mean to identify myself with a postmodern author or school, and I do not mean anything terribly controversial when I accept this claim. I understand the postmodern era to be the era which follows modernity, and to be the era in which there is a distinct lack of agreement as to what are the central intellectual concerns of the humanities. There was a time in the western intellectual past, call it *modernity*, when leading scholars in the humanities pursued modernist projects. The key feature of these modernist projects, which distinguished them from pre-modern intellectual activities, was their *humanism*. The great modernist ambition was that, instead of appealing to external authorities such as God, we humans would be able to generate our beliefs and values from within. Descartes and Kant are exemplary modernist philosophers, asking us to look inward, and let our own reason lead us where it may. From the nineteenth century onwards, intellectuals have become increasingly disenchanted with the modernist ambitions that drove their intellectual forebears. The age of postmodernity is characteristically an age in which this disenchantment is given voice.[1] What else the age of postmodernity is, is a matter of considerable disagreement. Such disagreements need not concern us here, however.

1.3 Flaws in the glass

According to Rorty, the reason why epistemology came to occupy the central place in modern philosophy is to be understood through appreciation of the *foundationalist* character of modern philosophy. For Rorty *foundationalism* is the quintessential project of modern philosophy. Although Rorty does not offer an explicit definition of foundationalism, it is clear enough from the ways in which he uses the term that foremost in his mind are systematic philosophies which take a certain type of epistemological justificatory exercise to be primary. Such justificatory exercises focus upon the structure of knowledge and make a sharp distinction between basic beliefs, or items of knowledge which are acquired by us directly from the world, and higher-order beliefs, or items of knowledge which are inferred by us from already established beliefs or items of knowledge.[2]

How did modern philosophy become quintessentially foundationalist? Rorty's argument, in rough outline, is as follows: After Descartes, modern philosophers have construed philosophy as a foundational enterprise because, like Descartes, they have been motivated to show how we can justify our assumed knowledge of the external world using only those resources which we find within ourselves. Unlike their pre-modern ancestors, modern philosophers were not satisfied with appeals to external authorities to ground knowledge claims. In modernity, the making of such appeals was considered to be a sign of failure to break with the superstitiousness of an intellectually inferior past. Thrown back on their own resources, modern philosophers became concerned to locate the proper foundations for genuine knowledge. This led to a preoccupation with representation. Show how we succeed in representing the world and, in doing so, it was hoped, you would reveal the epistemic foundations of worldly knowledge. Rorty, giving voice to the foundationalists he goes on to criticise, puts it like this:

> To know is to represent accurately what is outside the mind; so to understand the possibility and nature of knowledge is to understand the way in which the mind is able to construct such representations. Philosophy's central concern is to be a general theory of representation, a theory which will divide culture up into areas which represent reality well, those which represent it less well, and those which do not represent it at all (despite their pretence of doing so) (Rorty 1980, p. 3).

To support his claim that foundationalism is at the heart of modern philosophy, Rorty presents, in *Philosophy and the Mirror of Nature*, a grand history of philosophy in which adherence to foundationalist epistemological presuppositions is uncovered in a number of distinct areas of thought, including the philosophy of mind and the philosophy of language. Although Rorty does contend that the vast majority of modern philosophers have been foundationalists, his account of the dominance of foundationalism does not simply consist in sheer weight of numbers. Rorty views modern philosophy through the lens of what I will call a 'dominance/resistance' framework. As seen in Rorty's looking-glass, the majority of good and mediocre modern philosophers have been constructive participants in the foundationalist enterprise. However, a minority of especially talented philosophers, who began in this tradition, were able to see its inherent limitations and engaged themselves in resisting foundationalism's hegemony. The best of these resisters — and here Rorty mentions Wittgenstein, Dewey and Heidegger — came to recognise not only the failure of foundationalism, but the concomitant failure of any possible constructive philosophy.

Passing beyond the status of mere philosophers, and becoming great ironists, Wittgenstein, Dewey and Heidegger form a triumvirate of heroes from whom Rorty draws inspiration. According to Rorty, foundationalism has so dominated and distorted philosophy that we need a kind of therapy to enable us to heal the wounds which it has inflicted upon us, and the ironic works of the three philosophers mentioned somehow begin to provide that therapy. Although Rorty claims to draw inspiration from the works of Wittgenstein, Dewey and Heidegger, the actual cure he invokes to help rid us of the alleged burden of foundationalism owes very little to them but is to be found in a melange of more contemporary philosophy, including the holism of Quine, Sellars' attack on 'the given', the historicism of Kuhn and the writings of some recent hermeneuticists.[3]

Rorty attempts to persuade us that a monolithic foundationalism gripped modern philosophy from the time of Descartes until the middle of the twentieth century. However, a careful examination of his grand history of philosophy undermines the plausibility of this conclusion in at least two ways. The first of these is that foundationalism, which Rorty refers to as if it were one united intellectual movement appearing in different guises, turns out on closer examination to be a number of loosely related projects which lack underlying unity. Rorty associates foundationalism with the 'Descartes-Locke-Kant tradition' (Rorty 1980, pp. 8-9). While the first two members of this trio are conventionally described as foundationalists, Kant is a quite unlikely foundationalist. Broadly, Kant's response to Humean scepticism is to argue that the mind imposes order on the world. Such imposition, however constrained by the dictates of reason, appears to be incompatible with epistemic foundationalism. If we are in some sense creating the world as we organise our ideas about it, rather than finding Nature's categories, then our knowledge is not simply foundational. How then can Rorty consider Kant to be a foundationalist? Because he sees Kant as propounding a causal thesis regarding the constitution of the external world by the mind. Human thinking, insofar as it imposes order on the world, is foundational in the sense that it is a constitutive cause of the world and of worldly knowledge at the same time (Rorty 1980, pp. 148-55). On Rorty's view, then, Kant transforms foundationalism, from a search for the sole true foundations of knowledge, to a search for an account of the constraints on the possibility of foundation, while all the time assuming that knowledge is foundational in structure.

Ostensibly Kant has very different philosophical aims from Descartes or Locke. Nevertheless, Rorty has managed to interpret Kant in such a way as to subsume his philosophy under the broad rubric of foundationalism. If Kant can be so interpreted, one wonders if there are any philosophers who cannot be fiendishly interpreted as somehow extending or transforming a never-defined foundationalism. Because Rorty places no explicit limits on what is to count as foundationalism, and because he does allow so much to count, his claim of foundationalist dominance of modern philosophy is a fairly vacuous one.

A second undermining feature of Rorty's grand history is that constructive philosophers, whom Rorty does not attempt to describe as foundationalists, keep making unannounced appearances. If modern philosophy really was dominated by a monolithic foundationalism, as Rorty suggests, then all significant philosophers of the modern era would either be participants in the foundationalist enterprise or be actively engaged in resisting its influence, as Rorty's three ironist heroes are supposed to be engaged. Constructive non-foundationalist philosophy does not seem to have a place within Rorty's grand narrative of foundationalist dominance and anti-foundationalist resistance. However, *Philosophy and the Mirror of Nature* contains passing comments, about Hegel, Green and Bradley, none of whom would be easy to describe as foundationalists, and all of whom are normally regarded as the authors of works of constructive non-foundational philosophy.

Hegel is of particular embarrassment to Rorty, because of the extent of his influence and because he would be so very difficult to describe as a foundationalist, even given Rortian flexibility with the term. Hegel rejects the view that human knowledge, as it is currently constituted, is even coherent. On a Hegelian account, our present knowledge is shot through with contradictions, which will not be resolved until the end of history. If Hegel is right, then this undermines the foundationalist presupposition that items of knowledge which we have now, are or can be simply inferred from more basic items of knowledge. Rorty argues for the continuing hegemony of foundationalism, from the seventeenth century right up until the middle of the twentieth century, in both Anglo-Saxon and European philosophy. If the early and middle twentieth century is to be shown to be in the grip of foundationalism, as Rorty holds, then the nineteenth century had better not be portrayed as having significantly freed itself of that grip; and if Hegel and his followers were really as influential as historians of nineteenth-century philosophy typically depict them, then Rorty's story of found-ationalist hegemony lacks plausibility.

By most accounts Hegel's influence in the nineteenth century is strong. The 'Young Hegelians' disseminated variants of the master's views throughout Germany in the early decades. In the latter part of the nine-teenth century, the British Idealists looked to Hegel for inspiration.[4] Rorty attempts to recount the history of nineteenth-century philosophy in such a way as to minimise Hegel's influence. Of the German scene, he tells us about Kant, acknowledges Hegel in passing, and makes much of the 'back to Kant' movement of the 1860s, as if Hegel had been a mere hiccup in intellectual history (Rorty 1980, p. 134). Rorty then outlines an un-Hegelian sketch of the British Idealists, attempting to emphasise their Kantian heritage, at the expense of Hegelian influences which usually feature prominently in historical recountings of British Idealism (Rorty 1980, p. 147).[5]

Other names which could be cited to undermine Rorty's grand narrative are those of the Vienna Circle positivists, Carnap and Neurath. A once widely held view, which would have added to the plausibility of Rorty's grand narrative, if it were true, was the view that the Vienna Circle positivists were, one and all, foundationalists. Recent historical work by Reisch (1991), Uebel (1991), Friedman (1992a) and Earman (1993) shows us that by the mid-1930s leading members of the Vienna Circle had effectively abandoned epistemic foundationalism. On Earman's view, Kuhn, who is a revolutionary figure for Rorty, is a reformist extender of ideas which had already been explicated in the later writings of Carnap (Earman 1993). If an intellectual movement as significant as logical positivism, which flourished during a time supposed by Rorty to be dominated by foundationalism, is not in fact consistently foundationalist, then Rorty's grand narrative is further discredited.

Rorty invites us to see foundationalism as the cornerstone of modern philosophy by imposing a dominance/resistance schema on that history. Modern philosophers are either portrayed as participants in the dominant tradition, or as being busy rebelling against it. In order to make this story plausibly totalising, Rorty glosses over the differences between the various positions which he describes as foundationalist, and glosses over the differences between non-foundationalist positions. Crucially, Rorty avoids considering the constructive philosophy of non-foundationalists of the modern era such as Hegel, Green and Bradley. The fact that these significant philosophers of the modern era produced constructive philosophy that is non-foundationalist undermines the dominance/

resistance framework. The supposed resisters are clearly not gripped by the fight against a dominant tradition if they are shown to be concerned with the business of building their own positive philosophies. Perhaps the majority of modern philosophers were foundationalists. But modern philosophy outruns foundationalism. Rorty does show up a correlation between modernist thinking and the quest for absolute epistemic justification, as have others. However, he does little to show why that quest should necessarily take the form of epistemic foundationalism rather than, say, holism. Rorty attempts to portray epistemology as being irrevocably caught up with foundationalist modern philosophy. If it was, then the claim that epistemology is now dead might be plausible. However, as we have seen, the actual relationship between epistemology, foundationalism and modern philosophy is much too loose to support Rorty's position.

1.4 Epistemology in postmodernity

The final two chapters of *Philosophy and the Mirror of Nature* jointly constitute a speculative characterisation of postmodernist philosophy as free of epistemology. Or rather, they jointly constitute two intertwined, speculative characterisations of postmodernist philosophy as epistemology-free. Neither of these is sufficient to convince us that postmodern philosophers ought to abandon epistemology. The first, an appeal to hermeneutics, turns out to do away with epistemology in name only. The second, an appeal to the Kuhnian conception of incommensurability, could substantially succeed in getting rid of epistemology, if it was accepted in a very strong form. But, as I will go on to argue, it is untenable in such a form.

Hermeneutics without epistemology?

Although Rorty self-consciously resists the urge to name a successor subject to play the role which he supposes epistemology to have played in modern philosophy, he does identify a successor activity for unreconstructed modernist epistemologists to take up, should they become convinced by his arguments. This activity is *hermeneutics*. There is a sense in which hermeneutics is often thought of as a distinct activity from epistemology; a sense which hermeneuticists sometimes attempt to capture when they talk about the distinction between explanation and understanding. Put simply, the idea is that while epistemology is properly concerned with the study of scientific explanation, there are some subjects, notably language-using humans, which are said to be inappropriate objects of explanation, and which need instead to be understood.

Hermeneuticists have traditionally argued that the language-saturated sphere of human understanding differs from the empirical realm of the natural sciences in such a way as to justify a fundamental methodological rift between the two. This rift is generally referred to as the 'natural-science/social-science distinction', although Rorty refers to it as the spirit-nature distinction (Rorty 1980, p. 353). While scientific explanation is appropriate in the natural sciences, it is said to be out of place in the human sciences, where hermeneutics must supply interpretive norms. Early hermeneuticists, as well as their more contemporary intellectual descendants, have all wanted to insist upon a natural-science/social-science distinction. We will consider this distinction, the hermeneutic tradition and its legacy further in Chapter Three.

Unlike these more traditional hermeneuticists, Rorty does not advocate the mere separation of epistemology from hermeneutics. He advocates the abandonment of all epistemology in favour of hermeneutics. Unsurprisingly, Rorty has very different views about hermeneutics from the more traditional ones. Rorty's characterisation of post-epistemological hermeneutics is not developed in detail in *Philosophy and the Mirror of Nature*; however, one crucial detail which Rorty does include is that he calls for the natural-science/social-science (spirit-nature) distinction to be abandoned (Rorty 1980, p. 353).

Rorty is not alone in calling for the rejection of the natural-science/social-science distinction. Of late this distinction has been heavily criticised, its opponents attacking the positivistic characterisation of the natural sciences which the distinction implicitly supports. Unlike Rorty, most opponents of the natural-science/social-science distinction do not advocate abandoning epistemology. Instead they argue that we should abandon the strong distinction between epistemology and hermeneutics. These opponents of the natural-science/social-science distinction, who are sometimes described as 'post-empiricists', advocate various sorts of fusions between the epistemological analytical and the continental hermeneutic traditions (another topic to be considered further in Chapter Three). They insist that, just like the social sciences, the natural sciences have an interpretive aspect, and therefore that hermeneutics is not out of place in the natural sciences and cannot be wholly discrete from epistemology (Rouse 1987, Okrent 1984).

Rorty makes the mistake of thinking of hermeneutics as if it were the traditionally-conceived, epistemology-free activity, while dispensing with the traditional distinction which kept epistemology separate from hermeneutics. In the absence of a natural-science/social-science distinction, it appears that hermeneutics cannot be a genuinely distinct successor activity for modern epistemologists to take up if they were to abandon epistemology, because it is not exclusive of epistemology. Perhaps there is a way to establish that postmodern hermeneutics can be kept untainted by epistemology without the prophylactic of a natural-science/social-science distinction. If there is, then the onus is upon Rorty and his sympathisers to provide it. As it stands, Rorty's characterisation of hermeneutics as somehow distinct from epistemology is inadequate.

Incommensurability and epistemology

The second way of thinking of postmodern philosophy as being free of epistemology, presented in *Philosophy and the Mirror of Nature,* is one which is indebted to the early work of Kuhn (Rorty 1980, pp. 322-42). Rorty takes Kuhn's notion of the incommensurability of different paradigms in the natural sciences and generalises it to all forms of discourse between different communities. If we go along with Rorty, we can see epistemological activity to be effectively redundant as a result. Whenever it might seem that a matter of serious epistemological contention arises, there actually is no contribution that constructive epistemological reasoning can make to the resulting controversy, as the controversy is not rationally soluble, being the result of a clash of rival 'world-views', 'paradigms' or 'forms of life', which are incommensurable with one another. Different groups subscribe to different world-views. They can not and do not get together and rationally resolve their disagreements as there is no neutral ground where they can go to find rational resolution. That much is all that there is to be said when an epistemological dispute arises, so epistemology is now effectively redundant, being restricted to the unimportant work of resolving intra-paradigmatic disputes — or so Rorty urges us to believe.

Although Kuhn has convinced many of the crucial importance of contextualization in the comprehension of scientific concepts, the strong view of incommensurability, which Rorty generalises from Kuhn, is very hard to accept. It rests on a characterisation of world-views as wholly discrete and entirely coherent. Nothing less will do to exclude the possibility of reasoned arbitration between the rival points of view which are being conceived of as world-views. But very few if any people actually live in pure cultures, unaffected by the influence of other cultures. The characterisation of people as having completely discrete, internally coherent world-views, and having nothing rational to say to other groups, is a caricature at best, if it is meant to describe the general condition of humanity now.[6] Kuhn himself was pilloried for appearing to hold such a vulgar view in the natural sciences, and in a series of articles he attempted to clarify his position to show that, despite appearances, an extreme conception of incommensurability is not implicit in his account of the historical development of the natural sciences.[7]

Not only is the proposition that we inhabit discrete, internally coherent world-views unconvincing, it is inimical to postmodern sensibilities. Postmodernists typically espouse extreme scepticism about the meta-theoretic. In the words of Lyotard, the postmodern attitude is distinctive just because it is 'incredulous towards metanarratives' (Lyotard 1984, p. xxiv). World-views, as characterised by Rorty, are all-encompassing theoretical constructs, and therefore metanarratives in Lyotard's sense of the term. As good postmodernists, those who take Rorty's philosophy seriously and believe that they inhabit world-views ought to look for inconsistencies within those world-views. If Lyotard is to be believed, they will surely find these inconsistencies. Taking post-modernism seriously will result in the rejection of the totalising modernistic idea that we are constrained by all encompassing world-views. So taking postmodernism seriously means rejecting the use of this line of argument against the possibility of post-modern epistemology.

1.5 The continuing importance of epistemology

Unfortunately Rorty has managed to persuade many that epistemology really is dead. What I believe makes *Philosophy and the Mirror of Nature* so influential is that it taps in to a very common way of thinking about epistemology. It is not unusual for epistemology to be conceived of as a very narrow, exclusively foundationalist activity. This can happen when epistemological arguments are thought of, as they frequently are, as being employed solely to justify our use of the epistemic tools which we put to work in coming to know about the world — science, reason and the senses. Epistemology, it is widely supposed, needs to do just one thing to be successful; defeat the arguments which are directed at undermining our confidence in these tools, the arguments of the sceptic.

Metaphysics and the Disunity of Scientific Knowledge

For some modern foundationalists the role of epistemology in philosophy probably was thought of as being exhausted by the task of defeating the sceptic. However, epistemology, even for modern foundationalists, has a wider importance. Epistemological considerations are marshalled when we choose between rival beliefs, norms and methods. Are we to accept the Theory of Evolution or Creation Science? Are we to prefer the simpler of two rival explanations which are of equal explanatory power? Are we to abandon a theory in the face of disconfirming evidence, or make an alteration in an auxiliary hypothesis supporting the theory to accommodate that evidence? These are all questions with practical consequences which the epistemologist aims to address, and the answers to them do not simply fall out of arguments which are aimed at defeating the sceptic.

Those moderns who actually were foundationalists often supposed that the answers to the above questions did fall out of the project of defeating the sceptic. Typically, they did so because they presumed that there was one approach to answering those questions which deserved general assent. This approach was said to be the one pursued by *science*, employing *the scientific method*. On this view, reputable scientists practised *the scientific method*, which was supposed to come ready-made with a specific set of proper attitudes towards matters of apparent epistemic choice. With this presupposition in mind, it becomes understandable that modernist foundationalists might have assumed that the defeat of the sceptic addresses the practical epistemic questions, which I have raised, *en passant*, by vindicating *science*. This happy image of *science*, which was once so widespread, no longer commands much in the way of assent. In recent times the overriding trend in the philosophy of science has been to emphasise the differences between the various sciences, and philosophies which identify a single scientific method or identify science with simple global prescriptions are increasingly rare.

Because of a lack of shared ambitions amongst intellectuals after the demise of modernity, postmodernity is, as a matter of practical necessity, an age of tolerance. Intellectuals in the humanities who do not agree on background assumptions, and who do not countenance the use of naked force, cannot expect the unanimous agreement of their contemporaries on any particular issue. In contrast to the methodological, metaphysical, and other sorts of monisms which reigned supreme in modern times, the postmodern era is characterised by pluralisms. With all this pluralism in the air it would be extremely surprising if there was no work to be done in epistemology. We still need to decide how to adjudicate between competing epistemic points of view, if only to decide on pressing practical matters. We still need to decide which scientific projects are to be funded and which not; and we still need to decide how we are to 'weigh' empirical evidence in the courtroom. It is simply dogmatic, and contrary to the spirit of pluralism, to insist that the epistemologist cannot make significant contributions to these decision-making processes.

Accompanying the changes in the intellectual climate are concomitant changes in the foci of research within contemporary epistemology and associated fields. There is a concerted effort to integrate epistemology with other disciplines. There is contemporary work being done which shows how psychological insights can affect epistemology. Also there is much contemporary philosophy of science which looks closely at particular disciplines within science in order to draw epistemological lessons. Additionally, there is work being done which integrates sociological insights into epistemology. All of this work is epistemological, although it may not be immediately recognised as epistemology by those who were convinced that epistemology is only done in armchairs and is only concerned with defeating sceptics.

Although epistemology has changed, the distinction between post-modern and modern epistemology should not be overstated. Systematic philosophy, which was previously directed at defeating the sceptic, can still profitably be conducted with the more modest aim of developing abductive arguments for this or that position. So, the long-running debate between holists and foundationalists about the structure of knowledge continues; only now the protagonists should be seen as trying to provide the best available argument, rather than the definitive argument. Furthermore, attempting to defeat sceptics can still be a worthwhile activity. This is because postmodernists are still liable to fall into the traditionally modernist trap of advocating arguments which have global scepticism as a consequence. Consider, for example, Baudrillard's well-known scepticism about the occurrence of the Gulf War. Baudrillard's scepticism about this issue turns on a scepticism about the media so broad as to effectively be scepticism about perception in general. Baudrillard has not passed beyond the problematic of the 'veil of perception' which bedevilled Locke and motivated Berkeley's solipsistic idealism. As long as there are Baudrillards to play the role of the extreme sceptic, there will continue be a demand for epistemologists to continue to oppose universal scepticism.[8]

The continuity between epistemology in modernity and in post-modernity should not be surprising if we follow Lyotard, rather than Rorty and Derrida, in understanding postmodernity as being continuous with modernity rather than seeing it as breaking sharply with modernity. Although postmodernists abandon the search for absolute legitimation which was pervasive in modernity, they do not abandon the humanism which was central to modernity, and which distinguished modernity from pre-modernity. Postmodernists share with modernists a commitment to finding whatever intellectual underpinnings for philosophy we can within ourselves. In essence this is why, according to Lyotard, *'the postmodern is undoubtedly part of the modern ... not modernism at its end, but in a nascent state and this state is recurrent'* (Lyotard 1993, p. 80).

Notes

1   See (McGowan 1991, Chapter One) for a discussion of the relations between modernity, premodernity and postmodernity which I am substantially in agreement with.

2   Haack identifies three different, loosely related ways in which Rorty uses the term foundationalism in *Philosophy and the Mirror of Nature* (Haack 1990, p. 200).

3   More detailed summaries of *Philosophy and the Mirror of Nature* are to be found in (Haack 1990, Murphy 1981, and Philipse 1994).

4   Passmore (1957) and Hylton (1990) both contain historical accounts of the philosophy of the latter parts of the nineteenth century which bring out the depth of its Hegelian character.

5   The following quote from Russell, writing of the early influence of Idealism upon him (in the 1890s) , encapsulates an attitude common amongst the British Idealists and those influenced by them, an attitude which stands starkly in the face of Rorty's neo-Kantian treatment of them:

> I was at this time a full-fledged Hegelian, and I aimed at constructing a complete dialectic of the sciences ... I accepted the Hegelian view that none of the sciences is quite true, since all depend upon some abstraction, and every abstraction leads, sooner or later, to contradictions. Wherever Kant and Hegel were in conflict, I sided with Hegel (Russell 1959, p. 42).

6   Taylor (1990), develops a similar line of argument against Rorty in greater depth.

---

7   Sankey (1993), follows the development of Kuhn's characterisation of incommensurability after (Kuhn, 1962). He shows that Kuhn's later articulations of the concept of incommensurability do not give rise to the mutually incomprehensible paradigms of popular conception.

8   Norris (1990), includes a chapter-length attack on Baudrillard's global scepticism. Of course, Baudrillard is not the only postmodernist who can be accused of effectively advocating global scepticism.

2 Fundamentalism, Laws, Causes and Lies

2.1 Laws and causes

At the end of the previous chapter the continuity between modernism and postmodernism was emphasised, undercutting the sceptical consequences of postmodern thought. That postmodern scepticism has become so influential is itself something that calls for an explanation. The somewhat speculative explanation that I will offer for this influence is that there is a legitimate target, inherent in much of contemporary philosophy, which bears an apparent resemblance to those targets sighted by postmodern sceptical thinkers, and that this is intuitively sensed by postmodernists. Following Nancy Cartwright, I will refer to this legitimate target as *fundamentalism*.

Cartwright (1994) declares herself to be opposed to fundamentalism. I maintain that the majority of modern and contemporary philosophers have fundamentalist tendencies, and that it is the intuitive objectionableness of fundamentalism which fuels the fire of an overreaction against fundamentalism which is now manifested in postmodern scepticism. In this section I will introduce the topic of fundamentalism, through a discussion of the development of Cartwright's ideas. The reader should bear in mind that Cartwright has only recently seen herself as being opposed to fundamentalism, and her earlier work (Cartwright 1983, 1989) is overtly directed at different targets.

Before discussing the development of Cartwright's ideas it will be useful to briefly consider the related topics of *laws* and *causes*, as dealt with in the empiricist tradition, which will constitute a background to the discussion of

Cartwright as well as to subsequent discussion. Logical empiricists, in particular Nagel and Hempel, had developed a unified treatment of laws and causes which were neatly interrelated with the deductive-nomological account of scientific explanation, the cornerstone of Logical Empiricism. In the discussion that follows a familiarity with Hempel's deductive-nomological account (henceforth 'D-N') of explanation will be assumed (Hempel and Oppenheim 1948). Readers not familiar with this model of explanation, and its impact on subsequent philosophical discussion of explanation, should consult Salmon (1989).

The centrality to science of the concept 'law of nature' is part of a modern view of science which developed as the Aristotelian teleological view of nature declined. On an Aristotelian view the proper business of scientists is to discover the true essence of a thing being investigated; which is to understand its *telos*, the goal that its motion is directed toward.[1]The ancient Greeks did employ a notion of law in many of their explanations, but, unlike us, they conceived of laws as regulative ideals of behaviour. If a law could be accurately applied as a descriptive notion it was only because a particular set of objects were succeeding in approaching their *telos*. The Greek term *nomos*, often translated unproblematically as 'law', is more appropriately translated as 'rule'. Greek *astronomia* was not, as it is often supposed, an examination of the natural laws governing the motion of the heavenly bodies, but rather a set of rules for study and interpretation of the motion of heavenly bodies (Ruby 1986).

The Latin *lex* is related etymologically to the English *law*. It was originally used to describe the effect of the regulative ideal of reason upon sentient beings, and was not intended to be used to literally describe the behaviour of inanimate objects, either by the Romans or the Medievals. Aquinas, following Cicero, insists that, strictly, natural law is only applicable to the human realm, and talk of the participation of the rest of creation in eternal law is metaphorical (Ruby 1986, p. 345). This attitude was also to be found among natural scientists after the time of Aquinas and was remarkably long-lived. For example Robert Boyle, writing in 1682, presumed that the concept of law is prescriptive, and stated that he could not:

> ... conceive how a body devoid of understanding and sense, truly so called, can moderate and determinate its own motions, especially so as to make them conformable to laws, that it has no knowledge or apprehension of.[2]

The shift to the modern usage of the term 'law' was made as a result of influences that are associated with Descartes and with Hume. Descartes is instrumental in relating the idea of law to the hypothesis of divine legislation. Descartes supplemented the Biblical view that God legislated as to the state that nature was in, with the addendum that this legislation was conducted in one act via the laying down of a harmonious set of laws of strict regularity. In so doing he decisively extended the applicability of the notion of law to inanimate matter and provided a justification for the assumption that the laws of nature were grouped coherently in a single grand schema. God is supposedly mirrored by his creation, Man, whom God created in his own likeness. We can infer that God, like us, his creations, appreciates simplicity and order in the world, and created this world, *the* world, with these virtues in mind.

Hume persuaded many to conceive of laws as an appropriate subject for metaphysical auditing. His attitude of metaphysical austerity greatly influenced subsequent empiricist discussion of laws and of causation, and continues to influence contemporary philosophers. Inspired by Hume, a tradition has developed, which is alive and well today, in which philosophers reduce scientists' talk of laws, in so far as this is possible, to talk of particulars: 'a vast mosaic of local matters of particular fact, just one little thing and then another'.[3] Descartes and Hume represent two diverging tendencies in the heritage of modern philosophical discussion of laws. On the one hand rationalistic philosophers have sought to sanction the metaphysics of mechanistic-theological views of laws. On the other hand philosophers with more empiricistic inclinations have wanted to reduce laws to observed regularities in the world.

As with laws, the way that causal terms are employed in common discourse suggests that causal relations are something beyond that which we can observe. It would be uncontroversial to claim that the wind causes my wet clothes to dry on an occasion when we sense the wind blowing and my clothes drying. However, all that we can actually sense, in this example, is that the wind blows and that my clothes dry. We never sense the causing of my clothes to dry by the wind. True, we can speak intelligibly of 'seeing that' the wind causes my clothes to dry. But, what we mean by this locution is not that we literally sense the wind's causing the drying of cloth, but that, after we have learned to make a certain set of theoretical presuppositions, we can, without apparent effort, interpret our experience using causal terminology. There is, then, a sense in which we can learn to 'see' causes, but there is no literal sense in which we observe causal relations as they occur. Because causal concepts seem to invoke the existence of something

20

that is not reducible to the purely empirical, they have been regarded with suspicion by Humean empiricists as being irredeemably metaphysical concepts.

Hume made apparent the metaphysical depth of causal concepts, and convinced the majority of subsequent empiricist philosophers of the unacceptability of that metaphysical depth. Prior to Hume, empiricist philosophers had made free use of the idea of *causal power*. Locke included a discussion of causal powers in his *Essay Concerning Human Understanding*, (Locke 1959, Book 2, chapter 21) and Berkeley's argument for subjective idealism turns on the alleged lack of power in various possible sources of our ideas (Berkeley 1942, SS. 25-9, 69). The term *power*, which today sounds archaic, and to philosophers trained in the Humean tradition evokes an air of mystery, is really a very commonsensical term, and is entrenched in ordinary language. If I say that wind has the power to cause clothes to dry, I encapsulate the obvious idea that it is in virtue of some enduring property or combination of properties of the wind that my clothes become dried.

The idea of power can be used to accomplish an important task in causal explanation: it enables us to understand why causal explanations are exportable. An explanation is exportable if it can be re-applied in new circumstances. Suppose I am entitled to conclude that a particular gust of wind aided the drying of my clothes. I am not yet entitled to conclude that in other situations, where winds of differing force blow on clothes of differing permeability, wind causes clothes to dry. But if I was entitled to the claim that winds *generally* carry an enduring power to dry clothes, then I would be entitled to export *specific* causal claims about the drying of clothes by winds.

Hume eliminated the notion of power from his conception of cause. He insisted that all there was to a particular causal sequence was the conjunction of the event described as the cause with the event described as the effect. For Hume, a cause is contiguous in time and place with its effect, and it always precedes its effect. These two conditions are necessary but not sufficient, on Hume's theory, to allow us to attribute causal relations to the world. There is a third condition, which is perhaps the most important. In order for us to reliably attribute causal relations to the world, a type of cause must be 'constantly conjoined' with the type of effect which it produces. So, on Hume's view, we are entitled to refer to wind as a cause of the drying of clothes only when the presence of wind has been invariably correlated with the drying of clothes.

There are two closely related sources of dissatisfaction with Hume's 'regularity' view of causation. First, because a regularity view of causation has it that all there are to causal relations are observed regularities between types of causes and types of effects, it fails to do something which the attribution of enduring causal powers could do — explain why observed causal relations should continue to be repeated. It also leaves us without proper grounds to export previously learned causal claims into new situations.

Second, the regularity view deprives the causal relation of any quality of necessity. Before Hume the attribution of the quality of necessity to causal relations was taken to be unproblematic. Hume pointed out that there are no logical grounds upon which to infer that the connection between a type of cause and a type of effect is ever necessary, given the sort of information that is available to us when we make causal claims. No matter how many times we have observed wind constantly conjoined with the drying of clothes, there are no logical grounds upon which to rule out the possibility that the next time I put my clothes out to dry, the wind will in fact cause them to become wetter, or for that matter, cause them to be transubstantiated into aluminium.

Hume's analysis of causation focused philosophers' attention on a sceptical problem raised by the apparently irreconcilable gap between the epistemology and the ontology of causation. According to Hume, we are entitled to attribute causal relations to the world only on the basis of observed regularities; and from these we are never entitled to infer that causes are necessary — at least, not *logically* necessary. But if we require that necessary causal regularities exist as a precondition for the possibility of causal relations continuing to obtain, then we require knowledge that causes are necessary; knowledge which we have reason to believe we cannot attain.

The supposition that there are enduring causal laws of nature in the world looks like a promising candidate to justify the common assumption that causal relations are (physically) necessary, and in recent times philosophers have often looked to laws of nature to address the inadequacies in the Humean regularity view of causation. Although we take the term *law of nature* for granted as a central explanatory tool in natural science, there is a lack of consensus among philosophers as to how to precisely define a law of nature. Three features of laws of nature are generally agreed upon, though. Laws of nature are universal, relational, and differ from mere regularities in that they are projectable. Universality is consistency across space and time; and it is usually considered that a genuine law of nature must hold true at all times and places (it will become clear later that this is not how I will understand laws). Laws of nature are relational in that they express regularities that hold between elements of two or more classes of objects or properties of objects. It is membership of one or more of these classes that enables an object or its properties to be subject to a law of nature.

Scientists' confidence in the projectability of their generalisations is reflected in their referring to those generalisations as 'laws of nature'. Set with the conviction that they were doing science, or perhaps 'meta-science', rather than speculative metaphysics, early twentieth-century positivist philosophers struggled to reconcile their desire to do justice to science as it was practised with their desire to keep faith with their metaphysically austere empiricist heritage. The scientific notion of a law of nature appears to be blatantly and unreconstructably metaphysical. It suggests that there is something knowable, out in the world, over and above the regularities which we happen to observe, acting to structure those regularities. In the face of this tension, the move from positivism to logical empiricism can be seen as a compromise. Logical empiricists such as Hempel and Nagel tried to remain loyal to the positivist ideal of metaphysical austerity by being more modest about the ease with which they could expect to attain this ideal than the Vienna Circle positivists had been. They accepted laws of nature as a needed component of scientific explanations, along with a promissory note that laws could be rendered metaphysically toothless in the future.

In broad outline the programme for making the concept of scientific law safe for empiricist usage that was undertaken by the logical empiricists is a variant of the programme of Humean supervenience. Tooley (1987, p. 29), following Lewis, identifies that which is distinctive in Humean supervenience with the following two theses:

Thesis 1: The truth values of nomological statements are logically determined by the truth values of non-nomological statements about particulars.

Thesis 2: The truth values of all singular causal statements are logically determined by the truth values of statements of causal laws, together with the truth values of non-causal statements about particulars.

It is implicitly assumed in these definitions that particulars are discrete local entities and that all the causally efficacious properties which are instantiated in the world are instantiated in particulars.

The Logical Empiricist's method of finessing the problem of the metaphysical character of laws, and hence of causes, is embodied in

Tooley's Thesis 1. It amounts to the proposal that, in the final analysis, laws are nothing more than regularities among particulars. On this view, non-nomological facts about particulars determine all the facts of the world that there are, and thereby fix the facts about the laws of the world. In fact, the logical empiricist version of the thesis is stronger than the term 'Humean supervenience' suggests. The concept of supervenience was not in widespread usage at the time that logical empiricism was being developed, and logical empiricists generally thought in terms of reduction rather than supervenience. For them, facts about laws were not merely determined by, but were, in principle, completely reducible to, facts about the world. Given the explanatory framework of Humean supervenience, laws could be legitimately used in scientific explanation because in the ideal case where we had complete information available about the world, laws would be no different from regularities. In the ideal case the problem of projectability of regularities would not arise, because when all the facts are in there is no more projecting of laws to be done. Laws were legitimate explanatory tools for metaphysically austere empiricists, because they could be thrown away at the 'end of science', where they would be nothing more than regularities.

2.2 She fought the laws

In examining Cartwright's thinking before her identification of herself as an opponent of fundamentalism, we will be concerned principally with two books. The first of these is *How the Laws of Physics Lie* (Cartwright 1983, henceforth *How the Laws...*). *How the Laws...* is a collection of essays, organised around a set of closely related themes. Together these essays constituted an attack on scientific realism. The second book is *Nature's Capacities and Their Measurement* (Cartwright 1989, henceforth *Nature's Capacities...*). *Nature's Capacities...* deepens and strengthens Cartwright's arguments of six years earlier. It also shifts their focus. Instead of being directed against scientific realism, the arguments in *Nature's Capacities...* are directed against logical empiricism, and more generally against the Humean tradition. As we will see, in the mid-1990s the focus of Cartwright's arguments shifted once again.

In *How the Laws...* Cartwright's arguments are directed at establishing three inter-related arguments (Cartwright 1983, pp. 3-4). These arguments are:

Fundamentalism, Laws, Causes and Lies

(1) The manifest explanatory power of fundamental laws does not argue for their truth.

(2) In fact the way they are used in explanation argues for their falsehood. We explain by *ceteris paribus* laws, by composition of causes, and by approximations that improve on what the fundamental laws dictate. In all of these cases the fundamental laws patently do not get the facts right.

(3) The appearance of truth comes from a bad model of explanation, a model that ties laws directly to reality.

Cartwright's anti-realism about fundamental laws is a highly unusual position in contemporary philosophy. Anti-realism in the twentieth century comes in two main varieties. The first is instrumentalism, in which it is denied that we need commit ourselves to either the truth of our best theoretical explanations or of the existence of theoretical (unobservable) entities. The second is representational anti-realism, in which it is denied that there are truths about an external world independent of our representations of the world. A recent advocate of the second view is Hilary Putnam (1981). In many ways Cartwright is closer to the modern scientific realist than either of these sorts of modern anti-realists. She is willing to accept the (external) truth of many of the laws that science gives us, along with the existence of unobservable theoretical entities.

What is distinctive about Cartwright's position in *How the Laws...* is that she manages to combine realism about what she refers to as *phenomenological laws* of science with anti-realism about *fundamental laws*. The phenomenological is often contrasted with the theoretical by philosophers. Instrumentalists sometimes employ this contrast and map the divide between the phenomenal and the theoretical onto the observable-unobservable distinction. Cartwright does not use the term 'phenomenological' in this sense. For her, phenomenological laws are laws which directly describe the behaviour of entities in the world.

Cartwright accepts that science has given us immense numbers of highly confirmed phenomenological laws. Such phenomenological laws are laws directly describing the behaviour of concrete worldly objects. She emphasises the extent to which ordinary, common or garden phenomenological laws stand up to our scrutiny without requiring the backing of abstract fundamental laws to make them true. As an example of a phenomenological law, Cartwright cites Fick's law (Cartwright 1983, pp. 63-4). It is a law which relates the diffusion velocity of a component in a mixture to the gradient of its density. What we need to obtain Fick's law is sufficient laboratory time spent manipulating different mixed liquids. Here Cartwright concurs with Hacking (1983) in emphasising the way in which our ability to manipulate an object and intervene in its activity allows us to gain accurate causal information about that object. The phenomenological laws that we discover as a result are laws that we have good reason to be confident of being true because they are simply summaries of exhaustive investigations into the causal relations which an object of investigation has participated in.

Causal explanation, for Cartwright, is not a form of explanation which can be expected to satisfy the strictures of the D-N account of explanation (which is an account of explanation which she rejects, in any case). This is because, she believes, contrary to Humeans, that we do not typically accept scientific causal claims as a result of establishing patterns of predictions and confirmations to underwrite invariant evidential regularities. Rather, we typically come to accept causal claims as a result of manipulating entities and intervening in their activity in controlled situations (such as laboratories). This allows us to be justified in believing that entities exist, without being committed to the theoretical context in which their claims to existence are supported. We may not be sure what atoms look like, which model of the atom to accept as true, or exactly how atoms are composed of lesser particles, but nevertheless we are sure that atoms exist. Belief in their existence is warranted as a result of exhaustive experimental manipulation and intervention, resulting in a network of well-tested causal claims, in which atoms are sometimes cause and sometimes effect.

As Cartwright sees it, fundamental laws are very different from phenomenological laws like Fick's law. For her, fundamental laws do not describe real entities. Instead, they are about the behaviour of abstract entities in situations idealized from the complexity of reality. An obvious example is the universal law of gravity, which states that, for any two bodies, each body exerts a force of attraction on the other, directly proportional to the product of their masses, and inversely proportional to the square of the distance between them. This law might be true of ideal masses, but it is not strictly *known* to be true of all real objects. In fact, it is not known to be true of any real objects because we can never get a situation in the real world where we can isolate a particular instance of attraction between two bodies. This is because, according to the universal law of gravity, every body in the universe exerts a force of gravitational attraction on every other, and so interferes with our attempts to isolate any given instance of gravitational attraction.

Fundamentalism, Laws, Causes and Lies

A more important problem that prevents us from locating simple true laws is that the world is, in appearance, a complex sort of a place, and other factors are usually present that interfere with our attempts to isolate particular regularities. In addition to believing in the universal law of gravity, we also believe that many real entities are electrically charged, and that forces of attraction and repulsion between charged bodies will interfere with the effect of gravitation. Fundamental laws, which are traditionally thought of as being applicable without qualification, have an implicit ceteris paribus modifier in front of them, or more accurately a ceteris *absentibus* modifier: strictly, they are true only when all other potential interfering factors are absent. Fundamental laws are idealized generalisations abstracted from real circumstances. Although the real circumstances which they are abstracted from may be truly described, these idealized laws are not themselves underwritten by manipulation and intervention, therefore for Cartwright they cannot be reliable sources of causal information about real entities.

In sharp contrast to phenomenological laws which have a primarily descriptive function, fundamental laws have a unificatory-explanatory function. Fundamental laws draw together differing phenomenal laws, to create overarching theories. These theories explain rather than merely describe. As Duhem (1954) emphasised, theories comprised of fundamental laws are mathematical abstractions from experimental data, not descriptions of that data. Not only do fundamental laws not have to be true in order to fulfil their explanatory function, according to Cartwright they are often better suited for explanatory success if they are false, if they are ideal rather than actual. By being about ideal situations rather than real ones, laws can be simpler and therefore more easily applied to a far greater range of cases. The very falsity of fundamental laws is a potential source of their explanatory power.

According to Cartwright it is important for our explanatory purposes that we do tolerate falsehood in fundamental laws. This is because, as far as we can tell, true laws are scarce in nature, and in order to endow our scientific explanations with generality we often have to settle for approximate explanations. Laws will truly explain a small range of phenomena under ideal conditions, but they will approximately explain a large number of phenomena under a wide range of less than ideal conditions (Cartwright 1983, pp. 46-9). For example, Snell's law is a well-established law which describes the change in direction which rays of light undergo when they propagate through different media. The angle of refraction of light may be derived using an equation which is typically presented in science texts as being applicable to all media without qualification. In fact, however, Snell's law only holds true for any two media that are isotropic (having a uniform index of refraction), and most actual media are anisotropic (Cartwright 1983, p. 47). We don't have laws that describe the behaviour of light in anisotropic media, but we know that the behaviour of light in anisotropic media usually approximates to that of light in isotropic media, and so we make do with the ideal law which we have managed to identify.

The view of explanation at the fundamental level that has been outlined is Cartwright's simulacrum view of explanation. A simulacrum explanation is a model, idealized from reality. Fundamental explanations invoke theories which describe the detail of an ideal model, rather than the actual phenomena which the ideal model is then invoked to explain. Actual phenomena frequently fail to fit the descriptions which our ideal models would predict, and in the face of poor fit between models and reality, scientists tend to make local ad hoc amendments to models rather than abandon them. A study of the construction of models for amplifiers, due to Cartwright and Jon Norby, furnishes an example of this behaviour. Cartwright and Norby carefully detail the points where practice in the construction of amplifier models diverges from fundamental theory because of specific causal factors, showing how engineers approximate away from general theory in ad hoc ways, in order to achieve far greater descriptive accuracy than they would otherwise have obtained (Cartwright 1983, pp. 107-12).

We have seen how fundamental laws can be explanatory but not true (Cartwright's Argument 1), and how the way in which they are used in explanation argues for their falsehood (Argument 2). I will now explain the third argument of *How the Laws...*; which was that realists were led to believe that fundamental laws were true because of the inadequacies of the model of explanation which they adhered to, the D-N model. Logical Empiricists, such as Grünbaum, Hempel and Nagel, argued for the D-N view of scientific explanation alongside a view of the world that accorded a privileged place to fundamental laws, which Cartwright refers to as the 'generic-specific' view.

On the generic-specific view, which Laymon calls the 'priority thesis' (Laymon 1989, p. 353), the specific phenomenal laws which we happen to find, are true in so far as they are a consequence of the interaction of a complete and coherent set of generic fundamental laws. Grünbaum encapsulates the view as follows:

... while (a more comprehensive law) G entails (a less comprehensive law) L logically, thereby providing an explanation of L, G is not the 'cause' of L. More specifically, laws are explained *not* by showing the regularities they affirm to be products of the operation of causes but rather by recognizing their truth to be special cases of more comprehensive truths (Grünbaum 1954, p. 14).

This is the application of a Mill-Ramsey-Lewis style analysis of the concept *law* to science. Grünbaum and other advocates of the generic-specific view are not merely claiming that if comprehensive, fundamental laws are true, specific phenomenological laws which are special cases of them would be true. They believe that the fundamental laws of science really are axiomatic regularities of true scientific theories, or at least of our best confirmed theories, and that phenomenological laws (or very close approximations to these) can be logically derived from those axiomatic regularities in conjunction with statements of initial conditions.

In order to provide generic-specific legitimacy for our use of phenomenal laws in scientific explanation, fundamental laws need to be both general and true. The fundamental laws we might like to find would indeed be general and true, but the actual fundamental laws that scientists use in explanation do not conform to this ideal. The divergence between the fundamental laws that we might like and the ones we have is disguised by our use of implicit ceteris paribus qualifiers in the presentation of fundamental laws.

On the one hand, fundamental laws unqualified by ceteris paribus clauses are true only in a range of ideal conditions. Outside of that range, they are literally false. On the other hand, if we accept that a fundamental law itself incorporates ceteris paribus modifiers — if we construe the ceteris paribus modifiers to be parts of the law itself — then that law will be a vacuous generalisation unless the particular set of ceteris paribus modifiers is fully detailed, and this rarely if ever occurs in actual scientific explanations. Furthermore, if a set of ceteris paribus modifiers could be fully detailed, the resultant law would, in all likelihood, be a highly specific one, and not be sufficiently general for fundamental explanatory purposes.

Although the problem of implicit ceteris paribus clauses in explanation statements is a simple problem, it is a problem which really does threaten the D-N view of explanations.[4] On the D-N view, a law-like proposition is not a law if it has any exceptions, so laws with ceteris paribus clauses cannot be part of true explanations. But the fundamental laws of science *are* employed with ceteris paribus modifiers, so the fundamental laws of science cannot be literally construed as D-N laws. This is a swift but stunning conclusion and it raises the question of how it could be that Logical Empiricists ignored the idealness of fundamental laws, given that it very obviously threatened to undermine their philosophical programme. It turns out that the Logical Empiricists were aware of the problem, and thought that they had a quick answer.

To see the Logical Empiricists' quick answer to the problem of idealized laws, and to see how it is inadequate, consider the following example. Boyle's law, one of the ideal gas laws, states that the volume of a given mass of any gas is inversely proportional to its pressure (pV = const.). Boyle's law is true, at best, only for a certain number of gases, within a particular range of temperatures. Scientists know that it is not a true law because it does not take into account the effect of intermolecular forces within a gaseous body. In order to account for the effect of intermolecular forces when expressing the relation between pressure and volume of a gas, we need van der Waal's law:

$(p + a/V^2)(V - b)$ = const. [where a = the average intermolecular force and b = the total volume of molecules].

Laws such as Boyle's law, which are known to be false, are employed in explanations by scientists because they are also assumed to approximate to results obtained with the use of real empirical laws, within certain ranges of convenience, where they happen to be simpler to use. So idealizational laws are resorted to in science, but their use is explained away by Logical Empiricists as being incidental: a matter of convenience that is justifiable because they approximate to known true empirical laws.

This answer is too swift. Van der Waal's law, the law 'backing' Boyle's law, is applicable in a greater range of circumstances than Boyle's law, but it too is only the provider of approximations in actual situations, and is not, strictly speaking, true in all the circumstances it applies to. It neglects a range of other factors that contribute to the complex relation between the pressure, temperature and volume of real gases. Like Boyle's law, van der Waal's law is itself an idealizational law. We will discuss idealization at length in Chapter Five.

It had appeared to the Logical Empiricists that the scientific use of obviously idealizational laws was explicable by the approximation of ideal laws to true empirical laws, within certain parameters which happened to be convenient. On this account idealizational laws are portrayed as conveniences that are contingent upon the possession, by scientists, of knowledge of true fundamental laws to back them up. For adherents of the

D-N view of explanation, it is the supposed truth of fundamental laws which makes idealizations to them useful, and phenomenal laws true. However, for Cartwright the opposite is true. As she puts it, in a broadside directed against scientific realists, who have generally accepted the D-N view of explanation along with the generic-specific view of the interrelation of laws:

> Realists are inclined to believe that if theoretical laws are false and inaccurate, then phenomenological laws are more so. I urge just the reverse. When it comes to the test, fundamental laws are far worse off than the phenomenological laws they are supposed to explain (Cartwright 1983, p.3).

Many contemporary empiricists and realists are inclined to concede that the laws of science which we have now are deficient in the ways that Cartwright suggests, but want to insist that there really are a set of true laws, out there waiting to be discovered, which do not have these faults. Cartwright believes that realist apathy in the face of this objection is a consequence of the continuing influence of seventeenth century mechanical philosophy, exemplified by thinkers such as Boyle, Hooke, Newton and Descartes. On the seventeenth century view, the laws which science is seeking to discover are a divinely created, elegant set of coherent, comprehensive and true laws. Cartwright thinks, reasonably enough, that scientists should be open-minded about the substructure of the universe. It might be like that, but it might also be that the universe turns out to be a very messy place, in which some events are the result of a great number of interacting laws and where others events are less determinate, or even anomalous. To give us a sense of the difference between her position and the one which she is opposing, Cartwright turns to Duhem's distinction between the deep but narrow French mind and the broad but shallow English mind. The English mind:

> ... engineers bits of gears, and pulleys, and keeps the strings from tangling up. It holds a thousand different details all at once, without imposing much abstract order or organisation (Cartwright 1983, p. 19).

At the back of their minds, realists tend to assume that God has a French mind, inclined to elegant, coherent, simplifying and deep explanations. When theology was closely interrelated with science, we might perhaps have felt entitled to assume that God was French. But following the onset of the scientific revolution, we are no longer entitled to presume that theology is relevant to science, so we are clearly not entitled to make such an assumption. Unfortunately the dominant view of scientific explanation in the twentieth century has been predicated on just such an assumption.

2.3 The lies remain the same

In *Nature's Capacities*... Cartwright sees herself as being involved in a struggle against what she sees as the dominant 'Humean tradition'. At stake is the right to be considered the legitimate heir of empiricism. As we saw, the dominant logical empiricist approach has been to ground the key concept of 'scientific explanation' in projectable laws of nature. The logical empiricist Humean can then either argue that acceptance of the existence of laws is the right 'metaphysical price' to pay for an account of scientific explanation, or hold out the hope that laws can be shown to be supervenient on particulars and can thus be 'modalised away': portrayed as part of a description of the world but not as a part of the world as it really is (Cartwright 1989, pp 158-60).

Cartwright's strategy against the Humean, in *Nature's Capacities*..., proceeds as follows. She argues, reiterating points made in *How the Laws*..., that as a matter of fact we don't identify laws by finding exceptionless regularities in nature. If that is how you think you get laws, then you will find very few in this world; too few to build a plausible image of modern science. The fundamental laws of contemporary scientific explanation are idealizational, exceptionless regularities only after the messiness of reality has been mentally stripped away.

The Humean wants to be able to employ exceptionless regularities in explanations, and there is apparent hope that she can if she accepts the existence of causes. This is an additional metaphysical cost, but by accepting it the Humean will be able to put the nomological programme for scientific explanation back on course. It sounds like a good deal, but there is a catch. Cartwright argues that in order for causes to do the work needed, to endure outside the context of their discovery, and to operate in differing combinations in a variety of different situations, causes need to be understood as expressions of enduring capacities.

Capacities (also known as powers, dispositions, natures and tendencies) are ascriptions of enduring causal efficacy to objects and to the properties of objects. The Humean would read the phrase 'aspirin relieves headaches' as something like 'statistically, aspirin consumption correlates with a decrease in headache reports'. An advocate of the existence of causal capacities, however, would interpret the same statement to mean that 'aspirins tend to cause headaches to cease; but sometimes headaches will not be correspondingly observed to cease, because the causal power of aspirins is sometimes insufficient to relieve a specific headache, and is sometimes overridden by other factors.'

The Humean wants to provide an 'image of science' in a way that is metaphysically minimal. If we invoked laws to do the work, it turned out (if we accept Cartwright's arguments in *Nature's Capacities*...) that we needed causes and causal capacities to assist them; it doesn't look like a very promising strategy. Cartwright offers us what she takes to be a better one: accept causal capacities and try to do away with laws. If the Humean accepts Cartwright's gambit and admits causes, she will find herself at a tactical disadvantage when it comes to satisfying the metaphysical auditor — such a disadvantage, in fact, that Cartwright believes her own approach will come to be seen as the more attractive way to achieve metaphysical austerity.

In *How the Laws*... Cartwright argued in favour of acceptance of causal claims at the phenomenal level, but against similar claims at the fundamental level. In *Nature's Capacities*... she argues for acceptance of causal capacities at the fundamental level. Causal capacities are now to be accepted as being real in nature. This concession may suggest something of a capitulation in favour of realism about fundamental laws, which can be expressions of capacities, on Cartwright's account. However, in *Nature's Capacities*..., Cartwright emphatically reaffirms her anti-realism about fundamental laws, stating that 'fundamental laws are not true, nor nearly true, nor true for the most part' (Cartwright 1989, p. 175). One response to this apparent discrepancy is to suggest that she holds contradictory views. This is Alan Chalmers' reading of Cartwright (Chalmers 1993). However, Cartwright can be read in such a way that Chalmers' charge of contradiction is avoided. I will now show that she is best read that way.

Before launching into a defence of Cartwright we need to clarify the charge of contradiction. Chalmers puts it like this:

> In spite of indicating in the introduction that she is going to interpret fundamental laws as 'laws about enduring tendencies and capacities' she seems to contradict this later in the same introduction when she writes 'the point of this book is to argue that we must admit capacities, and my hope is that once we have them we can do away with laws' (Chalmers 1993, p. 203).

The contradictoriness of these two statements is not immediately apparent. Why would Chalmers conclude that they are contradictory? One answer to this question is that he is taking for granted the assumption that the relationship that capacities have to laws is that of truth-makers to truth-bearers.[5] On such a view, the fact that there are particular causal capacities in the world is what makes laws about those capacities true. This interpretation of Cartwright would seem to gain textual support from her discussion of phenomenological laws. Cartwright accepts phenomenological laws as true (or approximately true) laws describing the activity of causal agents, when we have successfully manipulated those causal agents and intervened in their activity. Analogously, she accepts that fundamental laws are about things causal, in this case Nature's capacities, which we are also justified in accepting as real because we have a proven ability to manipulate them and to intervene in their activity. Therefore, assuming an analogy holds between phenomenological laws and fundamental laws, Cartwright should be driven to accept that the fundamental laws of nature are true.

To defend Cartwright against the charge of apparent contradiction we will need to show that there is a sense in which laws can be about causal capacities other than the sense that is given by capacities being truth-makers for laws. A constraint on such a defence is that it must pick out features of fundamental explanation that are distinct from phenomenological description. This is because Cartwright does hold that phenomenological laws are true, or approximately true, because they describe real causes. If she is to hold that fundamental laws are about capacities and yet are not true, then they cannot be about capacities in the same way that phenomenological laws are. Fortunately there is such a sense available. It is this: Fundamental laws are not about capacities in the simple sense that they describe the behaviour of capacities in the world. Rather, fundamental laws should be read as licences to export information about capacities from ideal, simple circumstances to complex, worldly ones.

Fundamental laws, then, can be untruths about real capacities in that they are prescriptions for the misrepresentation of very complex worldly situations by the use of simple models that happen to be true of some very specific circumstances which we have access to, principally in laboratories. In the laboratory we can strip a piece of nature of enough of the component causes of a messy reality to be able to manipulate actual components of nature, and hence come to know of the capacities of those parts of nature as they truly are, in the absence of interfering factors. Unfortunately, such unmessy places where we can control and hence understand nature are few

and far between. We require simplicity for understanding; however '...
nature is complex through and through: even at the level of fundamental
theory, simplicity is gained only at the cost of misrepresentation'
(Cartwright 1989, p. 72).

We don't know how the capacities which we have identified in the
laboratory will react when interfered with by a worldly mix of other
capacities. Lacking that knowledge we make do, by assuming that
capacities will behave invariantly and are therefore representable as laws.
But strictly we are not entitled to this assumption:

> ... fundamental laws are laws about distinct 'atomic' causes and their separate
> effects; but when causes occur in nature they occur, not separately, but in
> combination. Moreover, the combinations are irregular and changing, and even
> a single omission will usually make a big difference (Cartwright 1989, p. 175).

In practice, what we do when faced with one of the frequent occasions
when fundamental laws fail to describe reality is plead interference, and
make additions and corrections to the fictitious fundamental laws which we
have imposed on nature.

So even though fundamental laws and phenomenological laws are both
about things causal, for Cartwright fundamental laws are radically different
from phenomenal laws in that they do not describe reality as it is. Instead,
fundamental laws give us prescriptions for exporting descriptions which
are true in one particular situation into other situations where they are not
strictly true. The supporting apparatus of additions and corrections, which
the realist about fundamental laws thinks of as true expressions of the
interference of other real laws of nature in the expression of a particular
capacity, are more often, for Cartwright, cases of ad hoc manipulation of
real data to make them appear to fit the predictions of the fundamental
laws that we employ. This story is unlikely to satisfy the realist about
fundamental laws, who will insist that experimental scientists discover
instances of true or approximately true laws, which are the immediate
source of real regularities behind the irregular appearance of the world to
us. It should be no surprise, however, that Cartwright adheres to it. This is
for two reasons. First, Cartwright is concerned to describe the process of
scientific explanation as it is practised rather than as it might ideally
become. Secondly, recalling an important theme from *How the Laws...*,
which Cartwright has not rejected in *Nature's Capacities...*, there is a deep
difference that Cartwright sees between the realist's presumptions about
the structuredness of the world and her own position.

Cartwright's English God does not organise the multifarious inter-actions of nature's capacities in a tidy way. There is no good reason to expect that there is a neat coherent statement about the interrelatedness of the laws of nature to be had. We make life easier for ourselves, by pretending that there is more orderliness in the world than God has provided. We do this by supposing that truths discovered in particular situations will remain true when reapplied in vastly different cir-cumstances. This is how fundamental laws can be false and be about real capacities. They are untrue generalisations about those capacities.

2.4 Anti-Humeanism

Humeans aim to provide an account of the possibility of knowledge, an 'image of science', while presuming as little in the way of metaphysics as possible. This ambition sets a standard for comparison of rival Humean philosophies. The more metaphysically frugal an account of science is, the more successful Humeans judge it to be. There are two points of potential vulnerability for Humeanism. First, we can question the worthiness of the Humean ideal itself. Second, we can use the Humean's own standards to show that the compromises which she has made in order to approach the ideal of frugality have a greater metaphysical cost than she is willing to admit, or perhaps show that she has no realistic prospects of recouping the metaphysical outlays that have been made. In *Nature's Capacities...* Cartwright pursued this second strategy. She attacked conventional neo-Humean philosophy in order to push for a new empiricism, while maintaining metaphysical frugality as a cardinal virtue.

The most metaphysically frugal accounts of nomic necessity, a topic which Humeans have typically taken to be the cornerstone of their images of science, are those derisively known as 'naive regularity accounts' by their detractors. These are direct attempts to build laws from regularities and nothing else. They typically involve making minimal restrictions on the type of regularities that may be considered laws. Such attempts fall victim to a host of well-known objections.[6]

Typically neo-Humeans have accepted that the 'naive regularity' approach cannot be sustained. More sophisticated neo-Humeans have followed two different paths to metaphysical frugality. Carroll (1990) refers to these as the *systematic approach* and the *epistemic approach*. The first, championed by David Lewis, and sometimes referred to as the Mill-

Ramsey-Lewis approach, is to restrict lawhood to generalisations that can be placed within the framework of an ideal overall system. The other approach, associated with Nelson Goodman (1983) and Brian Skyrms (1980), is to invoke epistemological considerations to limit candidate laws.

Lewis' account of laws admits only candidates that participate in an ideal account of the totality of empirical facts:

> A contingent generalisation is a *law of nature* if and only if it appears as a theorem (or axiom) in each of the true deductive systems that achieves a best combination of simplicity and strength (Lewis 1973, p. 73).

Lewis, and other systematist Humean philosophers, appear to proceed on the assumption that if we can construct such an ideal descriptive system of laws then we have described the true laws of a world. However, Cartwright as well as a host of other philosophers and sociologists of science show us that scientists do not assent to laws in virtue of regularities found in the world, at least not fundamental explanatory laws. A science that did proceed this way would be one far removed from our actual sciences. Against this line of objection the systematist Humean might insist that science does proceed in ways that, in some sense, approximate to the systematist approach. If we are living in an 'English world', a world which lacks an underlying set of governing laws, the systematist will attempt to maintain that the ideal systematisation of laws will turn out to be one which is not very simple, and possibly not very strong. Cartwright gives us reason to suppose that, because of the idealizational character of laws as they are used in scientific explanation, we might indeed be living in an 'English world' in which an idealized, false set of fundamental laws could be accepted because it is more explanatorily successful than its strictly true alternative. The systematist is mistaken if she believes that science as it is practised must approximate to the systematist approach. Actual science allows for the real possibility of simple and strong laws having explanatory power in an 'English world' where they are false.

The epistemic approach involves arriving at laws via appeal to personal probabilities. Scientists formulate hypotheses based on initial personal probabilities, which are then modified in light of the evidence of empirical tests. The task for philosophers using this approach is to match personal probabilities with what we hope are objective probabilities that could plausibly underwrite the evidence for laws of nature. A typical principle used to justify this process of objectification is the following: PR (P/Q) = r if and only if r is the degree of belief that an ideally rational cogniser would have in P given that he or she believed Q (Carroll 1990, p. 207).

Epistemic analyses need to explain why the objective probability of being a law (even if we can attain it) equates to being a law. Typically, they do this by having built into them some notion of resilience, aimed at capturing the invariance of laws.[7] It would seem that the definition of resilience and the specification of its scope will require some appeal to the way the world must be, a form of metaphysical commitment. According to Cartwright such a notion of resilience of probabilities, which is what Dupré (1993) refers to as a 'Contextual Unanimity Condition', is often illegitimately smuggled into Humean schemas. A thoroughgoing Humean can have no basis for belief in the contextual unanimity of causal laws. However, someone who believed in the existence of causal capacities would be entitled to appeal to contextual unanimity in arguments on behalf of causal laws because, as we will see in Chapter Four, the assumption of a notion of causal capacity is implicitly the assumption of the enduringness of causes across a wide variety of different situations.

Cartwright is right to argue that Humeans generally take on board more metaphysics than they care to admit. Systematist Humeans do this because they are unable to provide a viable epistemology that does not assume that the world is orderly at a basic level. This leads them to discount the possibility of an 'English world' in which it is possible for science to give powerful 'French' explanations. Inability to accept this possible state of affairs is, *de facto*, a form of unacknowledged metaphysical commitment. Epistemicist Humeans make a more direct unacknowledged metaphysical commitment in assuming the contextual unanimity of probability ascriptions. Either way, Humeans fall short of the ideal of metaphysical austerity.

2.5 Fundamentalism[8]

Cartwright's criticisms of Humean empiricism are telling, but in hindsight her use of them in *Nature's Capacities...* as the motivation for a rival version of empiricism which accepted metaphysical frugality as a desirable goal was a mistake. Cartwright had done nothing to show how laws could be reduced to capacities, and, as we will see, her recent work has marked a departure from this ambition. What needed to be rethought by Cartwright was her own commitment to the Humean empiricist virtue of metaphysical frugality.

Recently Cartwright has described herself as having been 'deluded about the enemy' (1994, p. 279), which she now takes to be 'fundamentalism'. Although the phrase 'I was deluded about the enemy' might suggest that Cartwright has dramatically broken with her earlier position, this is not how I understand her. It is my view that the opposition to fundamentalism, which Cartwright now advocates, was implicit in her work all along. During the late 1970s and early 1980s, when Cartwright was writing the essays which constituted *How the Laws...*, the realism-antirealism debate was at its most intense and Cartwright allowed her ideas to be pulled into its obfuscatory vortex. However she was never a straightforward antirealist, as her advocacy of entity realism in *How the Laws...* shows. Her position in 1989, in *Nature's Capacities...*, where she advocated the combination of antirealism about fundamental laws and realism about causal capacities, marked a further departure from the main traffic of the realism-antirealism debate. With the benefit of hindsight we can understand the development of Cartwright's philosophy as a case of successively refocusing her sights on a well-camouflaged target.

We can get a good sense of what Cartwright takes fundamentalism to be if we examine her account of what it is that she opposes. Her exposition of the characteristics of her enemy commences with a distinction — closely paralleling the distinction between fundamental and phenomenological laws, but of a more general form — between two sorts of law-like generalisations, '... (1) those that are legitimately regimented into theoretical schemes, ...' and '... (2) those that are not.' She continues:

> There is a tendency to think that all facts must belong to one grand scheme, and moreover that this is a scheme in which the facts in the first category have a special and privileged status. They are exemplary of the way nature is supposed to work. The others must be made to conform to them. This is the kind of fundamentalist doctrine that I think we must resist (Cartwright 1994, p. 281).

If fundamental laws literally governed this universe, then there are deep structural properties waiting to be revealed, the result of their governance. However, nature may lack the deep structural properties which our fundamental explanations attribute to it; furthermore, it may lack any deep structural properties. It is possible, on Cartwright's account of fundamental scientific explanation, that we can successfully explain aspects of the world by utilising the idealized orderings of our fundamental laws and theories, when those aspects of the world lack significant underlying orderliness. We might be living in a world where there are only local symmetries; a world of '... tens of thousand of patches, cut up in no particularly logical way, exhibiting tens of thousands of different regularities of countless different forms ...' (Cartwright 1993, p. 298) — Cartwright's 'patchwork world' hypothesis.

After noting that she finds antifundamentalist allies amongst those holding the antireductionist positions which are increasingly popular in the philosophy of the biological sciences, where there is a widespread concern to oppose physicalist reductionism, Cartwright makes clear that her opposition to fundamentalism goes beyond standard opposition to reductionism:

> Not only do I want to challenge the possibility of downwards reduction but also the possibility of 'cross-wise reduction' (1994, p. 281).

What she has in mind when she uses the phrase 'cross-wise reduction' is the exportation of fundamental explanations which succeed in some situations, into different situations — in particular the exportation of explanations based on fundamental laws, which accurately describe and predict the behaviour of idealized objects in abstract models, and may accurately describe and predict the behaviour of real objects in some contrived environments, such as laboratories, and perhaps in a few simple uncontrived situations — into more complex worldly situations where the veracity of those explanations has not been confirmed.

When Cartwright drops a coin from an upstairs window she knows where and when it will land. Newton's second law can be used to explain and predict the motion of the coin under the influence of the force of gravity, and the combined effect of any other causal factors which might be affecting its motion is insignificant. However, when Otto Neurath's physicist drops a thousand dollar bill in St Stephen's Square he has little idea where it will land.[9] Does Newton's second law govern the motion of the thousand dollar bill? If there is no known model in mechanics which accurately describes the motion of the bill, then it might be thought that the fundamentalist would be hesitant to answer this question. Typically however, the fundamentalist is not hesitant. Fundamentalists will usually argue that, although we cannot actually predict where the bill will land with any degree of accuracy, we could in principle, and we can therefore explain its motion by appeal to the systematic interaction of the combined forces of gravity and wind in a yet to be specified model. The fundamentalist, having been impressed by the explanatory power of Newton's second law, becomes convinced of its veracity, even in situations where there is a lack of evidence to support such a conviction. This is an example of the sort of cross-wise reduction that Cartwright opposes. The fundamentalist mentally reduces the complexity of the world to suit her favourite explanations. The possibility that Newton's second law applies to some types of objects but not to others is simply not countenanced.

Against fundamentalists, Cartwright (1994) maintains that, although we have evidence to support the conclusion that the bill is affected by the force of gravity, and we have evidence that the bill is affected by the wind, we do not yet have scientific reasons to hold that the wind operates via a force; and even if we did we would still lack systematic rules to tell us how to combine the interacting forces of wind and gravity in a model. So we are not in a position to assume that the motion of the bill is simply a product of the systematic interaction of forces.

In light of the foregoing exposition of Cartwright (1994), we can characterise fundamentalism as a metaphysical prejudice in favour of the existence of an underlying grand scheme — a comprehensive and coherent set of fundamental laws which govern the behaviour of all aspects of every entity residing in this world. Fundamentalists typically reinforce this prejudice by insisting that the fundamental laws that we employ success-fully in scientific explanations are somehow reflections of the fundamental laws that participate in this grand scheme which they suppose to be governing the world. That they are able to do this, is in large part because they ignore inconvenient details of particular circumstances where the veracity of fundamental laws is unproven or is apparently contradicted by evidence.

Presumably fundamentalists will concede that current explanations of the motion of falling thousand dollar bills are incomplete. However, they will not be overly concerned by this concession, insisting that the unpredictability of the motion of the falling bill is only to be expected, given the complexity of interactions between the forces of gravity and wind on a falling object which is significantly affected by both. The fundamentalist will insist that the forces of gravity and wind must interact in a systematic way which has yet to be discovered; and that this is most likely a complex way which cannot be represented in a linear equation.

The complexity of the systematic interaction between the two forces will be upheld by the fundamentalist as the best explanation of the varied and unpredictable behaviour of the bill on different occasions when it is dropped. Why does Cartwright want to resist this abductive inference? A short answer to this question is that she does not accept that appeal to underlying orderliness is a better answer than the supposition that the interaction between the wind and gravity is at bottom unsystematic. Although she would probably accept that the former answer is better in the sense of being more satisfying to us, she would emphatically deny that this makes it better in the sense of being more likely to be true.

Cartwright's opposition to fundamentalism is grounded in sentiments that seem to me to be very much at the core of the empiricist tradition. In a recent work Carruthers detects two main strands in the empiricist tradition, both of which have been used to differentiate empiricism from its rationalist alternatives. One is an opposition to the possibility of innate knowledge, and the other is an opposition to the possibility of any substantive knowledge of the world which is a priori (Carruthers 1992, pp. 3-6).[10] Another way of expressing the empiricist opposition to the substantive a priori is to say that philosophers and scientists ought to be open-minded about what the world is like, and willing to base their beliefs about the way the world is, as much as possible on empirical evidence. If there are to be no substantive a priori constraints on what is to count as worldly knowledge, then empirical evidence is, by default, the appropriate source of all worldly knowledge.

A fundamentalist is someone who has a mind which is not open; at least not open to the possibility of underlying metaphysical disunity. A thoroughgoing fundamentalist is committed to a very substantive a priori conviction that the world must necessarily be governed by a comprehensive and coherent set of fundamental laws. Other less dogmatic fundamentalists, who although perhaps not convinced that the world must necessarily be governed by a comprehensive and coherent set of fundamental laws, are prejudiced in favour of the hypothesis that the world is so governed being true, and prejudiced against the possibility of underlying metaphysical disunity.

The austerity of Cartwright's opposition to fundamentalism invites the charge that, in the end, she is simply an advocate of global scepticism; a charge which has historically dogged empiricists. In particular, it might be felt that Cartwright's accommodation of the possibility of metaphysical disunity makes global scepticism hard to resist. I think that open-mindedness about metaphysical disunity is relevantly different from genuine forms of global scepticism. To see how, consider the many scientists who profess an attitude of 'healthy scepticism' towards scientific laws and theories. By this phrase they signify an intention to accept laws and theories only after these have been subjected to the severest possible empirical testing. This attitude is not only reckoned by scientists to be fruitful for the development of good science, it is often supposed to be the attitude which is definitive of genuine scientific inquiry.

The phrase 'healthy scepticism' brings to mind the possibility of an 'unhealthy scepticism'. An unhealthy sceptic would be someone who takes open-mindedness so far as to end up championing global scepticism. An obvious example of unhealthy scepticism would be a scientist who is open-minded about the possibility that all earthly scientists might be 'brains in vats' being deceived into making false observation reports data by evil extra-terrestrial super-scientists, and who therefore concludes that the observation reports of earthly scientists are inherently unreliable. Clearly scientists need to put this possibility aside if observation reports are to be relied upon and scientific knowledge obtained. Empiricist scientists aim to let their beliefs be determined, to as great an extent as possible, by empirical evidence. However, the question of whether we are brains in vats is an evidence-transcendent question, one which cannot be answered by appealing to empirical evidence; so it is pointless for empiricist scientists, qua scientists, to concern themselves with it.

Cartwright's campaign against fundamentalism is relevantly different from unhealthy scepticism because questions of underlying metaphysical disunity, although very difficult to address, are not evidence-transcendent. Consider the choice between following a fundamentalist and supposing that Newton's second law is universally true, and the supposition that this law does not govern some cases, such as the case of the falling banknote. Here the barriers to evidential determination of belief are practical, not logical. If we were able to relate the interaction of the force of gravity and wind in a systematic way — a way which would provide us with vector equations to model that interaction — then we would be able to accurately describe the descent of the banknote and predict where it would land. If we were able to do this then we could empirically confirm that the force of gravity systematically affects the descent of bank-notes dropped in windy city squares.[11] If we are going to let our beliefs be dictated by evidence, as empiricists urge us, it seems that we ought to remain neutral about the potential applicability of explanatory appeals to the force of gravity in the case of falling bank-notes, in the absence of empirical confirmation.

Although the empiricist sentiments which I have attributed to Cartwright (1994) are austere, in one crucial respect they are much less austere than those of the majority of contemporary empiricists, which is that they lead to an attitude of metaphysical tolerance. The association of this attitude with empiricism will seem very unfamiliar to those who may have equated the Humean tradition with empiricism. Under the influence of Hume (as he is standardly interpreted), the dominant attitude towards metaphysics amongst empiricists has been one of making a virtue of frugality. To quote Price:

> The devout Humean takes the pinnacle of metaphysical virtue to be a world in which the only facts are the mundane first-order physical facts about how things actually are...(Price 1992, p. 387).

The dominance of the Humean ambition within the empiricist tradition should not obscure the fact that there is a rival role-model for empiricists, which is advocated by metaphysical pluralist empiricists. Metaphysical pluralist empiricists are motivated not by hostility to metaphysics, but by indifference. They retain the traditional empiricist concern to have their beliefs shaped by empirical evidence, but are indifferent to the metaphysical consequences of the beliefs which empirical evidence throws up. Metaphysical pluralists suspect that Humeans, in their eagerness to do away with causes and other metaphysically-laden concepts in science, gloss over the details of the empirical world, and insofar as they appear to succeed in their endeavours, do so because they do not properly acknowledge the idealized character of fundamental scientific explanations.

There is room in empiricism for both the metaphysically frugal Humean and the metaphysically wanton pluralist. What they both have in common, which unites them as empiricists, is an underlying ambition to ensure that beliefs are determined by empirical evidence insofar as this is possible; along with a concomitant opposition to any substantive a priori. This attitude is at the heart of empiricism. The Humean, often because of adherence to foundationalist and verificationist views about meaning, construes empirical evidence as 'sense-data' or in some similar limiting way, and then argues that one can never unproblematically infer from this 'empirical base' to the existence of anything beyond it. Metaphysical pluralist empiricists, perhaps convinced by realist arguments against Humean treatments of key metaphysical concepts, or by arguments against foundationalism and verificationism, reject Humean scepticism about inference beyond the 'veil of perception'. However, they do not reject empiricism in doing so.

Schiller and James strike me as fairly clear examples of metaphysical pluralist empiricists. Their arguments against Bradley's Absolutism parallel Cartwright's arguments against fundamentalism. Schiller and James hold that in order for Bradley to argue for the contradictoriness of apparent reality, and thereby motivate us to accept his arguments for its unreality, and the ultimate reality of the Absolute, he depends on general arguments about apparent reality which are in fact about an idealized version of that reality and which ignore the complexity and diversity of the real. It is only by idealizing away from the appearances of empirical reality that Bradley is in a position to set up arguments for Absolute idealism.[12]

In contemporary philosophy the most unambiguous advocate of metaphysical pluralist empiricism is John Dupré. Dupré (1993) describes himself as a 'promiscuous realist' as well as an empiricist. His *The Disorder of Things* (1993) is subtitled *Metaphysical Foundations of the Disunity of Science*. When philosophers speak of 'metaphysical foundations' they usually have in mind a small, coherent set of metaphysical concepts, the acceptance of which they advertise as the solution to many or all philosophical problems. Dupré has a different idea in mind:

> ... the disunity of science is not merely an unfortunate consequence of our limited computational or other cognitive capacities, but rather reflects accurately the underlying ontological complexity of the world, the disorder of things (1993, p. 7).

Cartwright is a metaphysical pluralist and an empiricist and in her recent writings this can be seen fairly unambiguously. Perhaps it would not be obvious to a reader who associated empiricism exclusively with Humeanism that Cartwright is or was any sort of empiricist. In the introduction to *Nature's Capacities...* Cartwright makes it clear that she does want to be considered an empiricist, albeit a very different one from Hume. She there claims to presuppose a 'strong practical empiricism' and advocates a return to 'an early form of British empiricism' which is in the tradition of Glanvill, Boyle, Hooke and Power (Cartwright 1989, pp. 3-4).

In *How the Laws...*, when Cartwright was 'deluded about the enemy', her commitment to a metaphysical pluralist version of empiricism had not yet been made, and she wrote as if she was a troubled Humean. By 1989, Cartwright presented herself as a staunch anti-Humean. Then, in *Nature's Capacities...*, Cartwright put forward a series of related arguments directed against Humean characterisations of science, arguing that Humean attempts to reduce causal concepts to nomic ones (with the eventual aim of reducing these to regularities) were a failure and arguing in favour of acceptance of a metaphysics of enduring causal capacities. However, she had not completely broken with the ambitions of the Humean programme at that stage. Cartwright had rejected all of the standard Humean strategies to satisfy the Humean's imaginary metaphysical auditor, but she had not abandoned either the desire to satisfy the auditor or the hope that the auditor might someday be satisfied:

> The point of this book is to argue that we must admit capacities, and my hope is that once we have them we can do away with laws. Capacities will do more for us at a smaller metaphysical price (Cartwright 1989, p. 8).

To my mind the point of that book was made very convincingly, but the hope was not advanced at all. The most likely explanation for Cartwright's retaining such a hope was a long association of empiricism with Humeanism. In her more recent writings (Cartwright 1993, 1994) she has decisively abandoned the residual Humeanism expressed in that hope and embraced a metaphysical pluralism which rejects the demand to count metaphysical costs.

2.6 Fundamentalism and realism

Cartwright's early confusion as to the identity of her enemy should not be surprising, given the widespread adherence of realists to fundamentalist views. Although fundamentalism is a common sin of realists, the influence of fundamentalism cuts across the divisions of contemporary metaphysics. Not all realisms are inherently fundamentalist, and at least one influential form of antirealism typically is fundamentalist. The view that there is a world out there independent of our thoughts, a view which stands at the core of realisms, may be a view held by many fundamentalists; however, there is nothing inherently fundamentalist about it. Cartwright is an antifundamentalist and her writings appear to presume that there exists a thought-independent world. A second form of realism, semantic realism, is specifically presumed by antifundamentalists. The semantic realist insists that theoretical terms refer to entities in, or aspects of, an observer-independent world; and are therefore made true or false by the way the world is. The antifundamentalist agrees with this stance, differing with the fundamentalist only on the epistemic standards required before we are warranted in assessing fundamental laws and scientific theories to be true.

Consider also convergent realism, the view that the natural sciences are capable of producing successively more accurate approximations to the truth about the world. Now, at first glance, it might seem that an antifundamentalist like Cartwright could not accept this form of realism. After all, Cartwright has railed against arguments to the effect that the fundamental laws are even approximately true. However, convergence realism is not incompatible with antifundamentalist thinking. Cartwright's objections to the verification of fundamental laws are practical objections, not in principle ones. It is the complexity of the world which threatens to defeat us in our quest for general theoretical truths, not anything more. Cartwright's objections are to what realists have taken to count as confirmation of fundamental laws. In principle, although perhaps never in practice, a fundamental generalisation could be accepted by anti-fundamentalists as a true law if it was sufficiently circumscribed by explicit ceteris paribus clauses so that it only generalised over those aspects of the world for which it was confirmed. If this is done, then, in the absence of antirealist arguments to the contrary, we are closer to the truth about the world. Cartwright does not argue against convergent realism, but for modesty about our progress towards the truth and for open-mindedness about what the truth is. I expect that the typical convergentist realist imagines that we have taken great strides towards the truth. Cartwright would argue that our progress has been quite minimal. Acceptance of Cartwright's antifundamentalist arguments would be seen as a severe setback by the typical convergentist realist, but that is not an argument against convergent realism.

Proponents of the above forms of realism can remain realists even when they become convinced by Cartwrightian arguments to abandon whatever fundamentalism may have been implicit in their realist commitments. In contrast to these non-fundamentalist realisms there is one influential form of contemporary antirealism that is deeply fundamentalist in outlook. This is what I will call constructivism (following Boyd 1983); a position grounded in the tradition of Kant, revitalised by the influence of Kuhn (1962), and whose leading recent philosophical advocates have been Putnam (1981) and Goodman (1978).

Constructivists allege that the theory-ladenness of our beliefs importantly constrains the possibility of realism about the objects of those beliefs. They hold that we do not observe or discover objects and kinds of objects in the world; rather, in some sense we project their form on the world, using our theories about the world to do so. We 'project the order of nature' as Kitcher (1986) puts it. Whereas the fundamentalist scientific realist holds that the truth of fundamental laws and scientific theories underwrites the regularities observed in nature, the constructivist holds that it is our acceptance of theories which makes us project those regularities. Because the constructivist insists that the world conforms with our theories, which are typically simple and general, produced for the convenience of limited beings, the constructivist is a fundamentalist. The possibility that the world is more complex and diverse than our theories allow is removed if we follow the constructivist in insisting that the world is importantly constituted by our theories. The constructivist antirealist and the fundamentalist scientific realist, although they differ about the direction of the relation between theories and observed regularities, share a fundamentalist presumption about the directness of the relation of regularities to fundamental laws and scientific theories.

As we saw earlier, Alan Chalmers (1987, 1993, 1996) has been a persistent realist critic of Cartwright. It will be instructive, given Cartwright's realisation that she is not opposed to realism itself, but to fundamentalism, to investigate the extent to which Chalmers' realism can now be reconciled with Cartwright's anti-fundamentalism. The issue to consider is whether or not Chalmers' realism is inherently fundamentalist or not.

Chalmers' main concern in his most recent discussion of Cartwright's work (Chalmers 1996) has been to argue that Cartwright's adoption of a metaphysics of causal capacities deprives her of any knock-down argument against realism about fundamental laws which she may have had. Chalmers concedes to Cartwright that at present we are only able to reconcile the apparently irregular patterns of variance of causal capacities in different circumstances, with realism about any particular fundamental laws of contemporary science — which might be used to explain the apparently irregular variance of those capacities — by ignoring the idealized character of fundamental laws. It is possible, though, insists Chalmers, that there are non-idealized true fundamental laws to be discovered which are made true by causal capacities that will one day be shown to vary in law-like ways. For Chalmers, an ontology of causal capacities, coupled with a certain optimism about the future direction of science, licenses realism about fundamental laws.

Chalmers' advocacy of realism about fundamental laws, together with his persistent opposition to Cartwright, might suggest that a description of him as an unyielding fundamentalist is appropriate. However, a careful examination of what Chalmers says allows a construal of his realism as being fundamentalist only in a very weak sense. Chalmers is a defender of a certain sort of realism about fundamental laws, but it is a highly attenuated realism. Unlike other realists who argue for realism about fundamental laws on the grounds that this is the *best* explanation of the success of science, or who argue, even more strongly, that any other view is simply 'miraculous', Chalmers is only concerned to argue that the fundamental laws of current science are 'strong candidates for the truth' (Chalmers 1996, p. 152). It would be difficult for him to argue for more on behalf of contemporary science because he wishes to hedge his bets about what the actual fundamental laws are like. He concedes that they might not be at all like the all-embracing laws that most realist-fundamentalists are pre-disposed to believe in. As he puts it, 'Holding fundamental laws to be true is compatible with the view that there are many such laws governing a very messy, very patchy world' (Chalmers 1996, p. 152).

If my interpretation of Chalmers is accepted, then his reasons for opposing Cartwright no longer hold. Chalmers' commitment is to the most general laws which happen to be true of this world. If these turned out neither to be laws which our currently accepted fundamental laws approximate to, nor ones which govern much of the universe, Chalmers would think this unfortunate, but would presumably insist that he wishes to believe in the true fundamental laws, whatever they may be, no matter how un-general they turn out to be. Chalmers is committed to fundamental laws in the weak sense of being optimistic about the discovery of some true laws which are fairly general. He hopes for the discovery of universal fundamental laws, and to the extent that his hopes lead him to underplay the importance of the possibility of underlying metaphysical disunity he is a fundamentalist. However, because he embraces the possibility that the most fundamental laws that there are are very un-general and consequently accepts that underlying metaphysical disunity is a real possibility, he lacks the main prejudice about what the fundamental laws are like which Cartwright identifies with fundamentalism. His differences with Cartwright boil down to a difference of opinion about the future direction of science, and philosophically, that is very little difference indeed.

2.7 After God's death

The fundamentalist presumption that knowledge must be orderly is deeply entrenched in modern and contemporary philosophy. Although this presumption was made by many before his time, its entrenchment in philosophy can be attributed to Kant. To understand why this is so we need to look at the development of modern philosophy before Kant and then forward again to see his influence.

For Descartes, God is the guarantor of the orderliness of knowledge, providing a divine guarantee that the mind, at least when attending to clear and distinct ideas, is able to produce an exact image of the true ordering of reality which God has created. In the Cartesian world God plays two explanatory roles. First, God makes particular thoughts indubitable, removing sceptical doubts about those thoughts. Secondly, God guarantees the orderliness of knowledge as a whole, so that armed with certain indubitable truths we are able to generalise to powerful fundamental explanations. Once God is removed from the Cartesian world-view, that world-view threatens to collapse. Most philosophers after Descartes ceased to employ God in the explanatory roles that God had played for Descartes. However, they looked for replacements, to fill God's explanatory roles on Earth; and they did this because they remained threatened by sceptical doubts, and they were inspired by Descartes' attempt to reduce the threat of those doubts by finding order in knowledge.

Kant's great contribution to philosophy was to suggest how the guarantee of orderliness might be found in humanity. For Kant, reason itself imposes order on reality. Kant promises us the desired guarantee of fundamental structure, at the cost of anti-realism. In order to explicate this solution to the problem created by the threat of disorder, I will now consider the Kantian interpretation of Hume, because it is in Kant's response to Hume that we find his response to the threat of disorder.

The Kantian view has it that Hume, the most important of the British Empiricists, is a 'friend of rationalism'. This is suggested in Kant's writings, although it is not made explicit there. It is a view that Kant's nineteenth century admirers explicated and which was accepted and propagated by idealists, particularly by Green (1894) in his commentaries on Hume. The view seems paradoxical; it makes perfectly good sense, however, if we accept that Hume, by presenting the clearest and most consistent variant of British Empiricism, showed up the muddied inconsistencies which earlier empiricists wound up being committed to. On this interpretation Hume showed, in particular through his treatment of causation, that consistent empiricism leads inexorably to a vicious scepticism. By demonstrating where a consistent empiricism would lead, and by inadvertently showing how unacceptable a place to end up that was, Hume's philosophy can be treated as one sustained reductio ad absurdum of empiricism.

Before Hume the categories of cause and effect had been treated as merely one grouping among the various forms of relations, no important distinction being made between logical and causal relations. Hume showed that causal categories were especially problematic. Whereas logical propositions, such as the fact that four is half of eight, were usually held to be knowable a priori, the relations between cause and effect were clearly not knowable a priori. As we noted in section 2.1, there is nothing inconceivable in imagining an uncaused event, or in imagining a type of event, hitherto always acting as a cause of a second type of event, suddenly becoming a cause of a third. Causation is the relation upon which our most important inferences about worldly experience depend, and it seems that in order for us to engage with the world rationally we need to be able to rely on our ability to infer effects from causes and causes from effects. It seems that we need to find necessary connections between cause and effect, but it also seems that we can never establish that we have found such necessary connections.

Hume-the-friend-of-rationalism's response to this predicament was his regularity account of causation. Perhaps the actual Hume held a view different from the regularity view.[13] However, mainstream philosophical opinion has it that Hume *did* hold a regularity view of causation, and that it was a view that could not be sustained for the simple reason (inter alia) that no amount of constant conjunction could provide the source of necessity that was requisite for causal relations to be as projectable as logical ones.

Hume-the-friend-of-rationalism is wrong but important. Important, first, because he shows how empiricism may be said to be refuted; and second, and more significantly, because he sets an agenda for philosophy to come. Hume-the-friend-of-rationalism directs the course of philosophy for the majority of both idealists of the nineteenth century and analytic philosophers in the twentieth century. This agenda is this:

First, distinguish sharply between causal and logical relations.
Second, establish that causal relations require the backing of logical relations.
Third, reduce causal relations to logical ones.

Hume-the-friend-of-rationalism would probably not have been so influential a figure had he not been first suggested to polite society by Kant. Kant accuses Hume of attempting to derive necessity from repeated association. Against Hume, Kant observes that derivation from constant conjunction can, at best, provide 'a merely subjective necessity' (Kant 1929, p. 44). For Kant, what is required to make causal relations respectable at the court of reason is strict universality. Reason itself must impose strict universality on relations. Hume's scepticism about causation is thus an important transitional stage, on Kant's account, towards his own critical philosophy:

Scepticism is thus a resting-place for human reason, where it can reflect upon its dogmatic wanderings and make survey of the region in which it finds itself ... But it is no dwelling-place for permanent settlement. Such can be obtained only through perfect certainty in our knowledge, alike of the objects themselves and of the limits within which all our knowledge of objects is enclosed (Kant 1929, p. 607, A762).

Kant thought of Hume's philosophy as a crucial step towards the correct way of doing philosophy, and ironically his own philosophy was to be treated in the same way that he treated Hume — by Hegel, the most influential of Kant's successors. Kant had taken Hume's sceptical analysis of causation and used it as the basis for an argument in favour of the view that the mind contributes to the construction of the objects that it observes. But Kant insisted that the external world, in his terminology the *noumenal* world, also contributed something to the makeup of the world as we observed it, the *phenomenal* world. But how could this contribution be made except via causal relations, which Kant had insisted were the constructs of mind? Kant had compared reason to a closed sphere constituted by our experience, and insisted that there could be no objects of reason outside of this sphere (Kant 1929, p. 608). By his own line of argument the noumenal world could not be efficacious upon the phenomenal world without our conscious assistance; but how could we consciously assist the activity of the noumenal world while we could not know of the workings of that world?

Kant's project was aimed at establishing the limits of reason, and perhaps it is his pervasive sense of modesty about the very possibility of philosophy which held him back from accepting the idealist conclusion that there was nothing that could be of explanatory significance beyond the phenomenal world. Hegel was not so modest, however, and was willing to follow this line of argument where it led.

For the idealists, causal relations were reduced to logical relations by the transformation of all relations into a special type of logical relation: the mereological relation between parts and the whole of Spirit or Mind or the Absolute. The way in which this reduction was to be effected was by means of a twofold strategy. First, the various different branches of human knowledge in which logical relations were employed in explanation were shown to suffer from contradictions. Secondly, these contradictions were held to be soluble, by a process of being recast and subsumed under new forms, as knowledge progressed by a type of unification: the unfolding of the dialectic. The point to which this process was directed was one where the contradictions, said to be found in apparent relations, were finally resolved into the mereological relations between parts and the whole of the final incarnation of the Absolute.

Kant had supposed that reason would be capable of imposing order on the world as a whole through its ability to structure the phenomenal world. The idealists looked at the phenomenal world and saw contradictions where order would have been, had Kant been right. Instead of abandoning the presumption that knowledge was ordered, the idealists held that there was logical structure, without contradiction, in the Absolute. The task of the philosopher, then, was to relate the world of appearance — now a world laden with contradictions — to the world as it would be if the Absolute were realised. Idealists could present a form of orderliness flexible enough to accommodate the appearance of contradiction — the appearance of disorder — provided that they could convince us that these contradictions would be resolved in the Absolute, where the underlying orderliness of knowledge would be fully realised.

I have put forward the speculative thesis that, following Hume and Kant, the directions in which modern philosophy has moved may be better understood if we see philosophers as searching for a level of explanation where everything is supposed to be orderly: a fundamental level of being in which to anchor our explanatory practices. Cartwright is right to complain about fundamentalism concerning laws of nature predominating among contemporary analytic philosophers. However, fundamentalism is a tendency which has deep roots in a sustained philosophical quest for order. Nietzsche may be right that 'God is Dead', but God's explanatory work on Earth has continued to be the preoccupation of generation after generation of philosophers.

Notes

1   Losee provides a simple exposition of the requirements of Aristotelian explanation (1993, pp. 5-15).
2   Quoted in Ruby (1986, p. 341).
3   These are Lewis's words. See (Lewis, 1986, p. ix).
4   Hempel (1988) confirms the seriousness of the problem of ceteris paribus clauses, which in his terminology are *provisos*.
5   In a subsequent paper Chalmers confirms that this is how he understands capacities to relate to laws (Chalmers, 1996).
6   See Armstrong (1983, pp. 1-73) for discussion of the naive regularity approach and objections to it.
7   See Skyrms (1980, pp. 11-12) on the definition of resiliency.
8   This section and a part of section 2.6 are taken from a separate paper 'Cartwright on Fundamentalism: Unmasking the Enemy'.
9   These examples are discussed in (Cartwright 1994, pp. 280-5).

[10] Carruthers (1992) goes on to argue that empiricist opposition to innate knowledge should be abandoned, but that contemporary empiricists should retain their opposition to the substantive a priori.

[11] In her earlier work Cartwright had further objections to vector addition (Cartwright 1983, pp. 54-73). However, these objections appear to have been motivated by Humean sentiments of metaphysical austerity which are at odds with the metaphysical pluralism to which she now subscribes, so I take it that they have been abandoned.

[12] This characterisation of the relationship between Schiller and James on the one hand, and Bradley on the other, is taken from (Wahl, 1925).

[13] See Strawson (1989) and Wright (1983) for interpretations of Hume that diverge from the mainstream.

3 Pluralism

3.1 Pluralism and anti-fundamentalism

How is the business of philosophy to proceed if we are anti-fundamentalists and eschew all restrictions on the ways in which we are willing to entertain the world as being ordered or lacking in order? We will be pluralists about both metaphysics and epistemology. Metaphysical pluralism follows straightforwardly from anti-fundamentalist open-mindedness. In the absence of empirical evidence to the contrary we should be willing to entertain the possibility that there exists any number of types of entity as well as any possible organisation of those types of entities in the world. Epistemic pluralism follows from metaphysical pluralism. If there is any number of types of possible entity and any possible organisation of those entities in the world, then there may well be a diversity of different methods that will turn out to be the most appropriate to the discovery of the behaviour of those entities.

Pluralism is currently fashionable in a broad spectrum of the different areas of philosophy. However, there is no overriding reasoning behind the current turn to pluralism, other than a popular sense that intellectual fashions change and that monistic approaches to philosophy have 'had their day'. Many contemporary pluralists are happy to confine their pluralist inclinations to one sphere or other, going along with epistemic or moral pluralism, for example, but balking at metaphysical pluralism.

The relation between anti-fundamentalist metaphysical pluralism and these limited pluralisms can be cast as analogous to the relationship between Hegel and Kant. Hegel accepted Kant's 'Copernican revolution'. Worldly objects are made to conform to reason rather than the other way around. But Hegel is willing to take Kant's philosophy one step further, and turns reason onto itself, thereby destroying the a priori categories that Kant had derived from reason and applied to the world. Antifundamentalist thinking, in some ways anticipated by Hegel, involves accepting the pluralist's recognition of the failure of philosophical monisms, but also involves urging that these be taken further. Epistemic, moral and other monisms were supported by metaphysical monisms. Just as philosophers should abandon their search for a priori restrictions on what might or might not count as an appropriate method for investigating the world or an appropriate means of making moral judgements about worldly behaviour, so too philosophers should drop their insistence on a priori restrictions on how the world might be constituted.

The sort of considerations which I have put forward are similar to the sort of considerations that postmodernists, such as Rorty, appear to accept as premises warranting sceptical conclusions about the possibility of constructive philosophy. Rorty, and other postmodern sceptics, argue that our failure to find certain knowledge equates to the failure of all attempts to obtain knowledge.[1] I am not so pessimistic. As I argued in Chapter One, useful knowledge does not require the foundations which Rorty argues that we fail to locate. Nor do I want to insist that there cannot be abductive arguments in favour of particular foundationalisms. An antifundamentalist attitude involves opposition to fundamentalist presumptions because they are currently unwarranted, not because they necessarily lack warrant.

3.2 Explanation and understanding

A promising place to start looking to see how antifundamentalist philosophy might proceed, while avoiding Rortian sceptical conclusions, is in the direction of the hermeneutical tradition. Recall from Chapter One that Rorty (1980) urged us to cease concerning ourselves with epistemology and take up hermeneutics. Mainstream hermeneuticists have offered similar advice, at least in regard to the human sciences. However, they have typically seen hermeneutics as a more constructive enterprise than the version of hermeneutics advocated by Rorty.

Hermeneutics is a term that was originally applied to the interpretation of Biblical scripture. The utility of the term was broadened in the nineteenth century by Droysen, Dilthey and others, who argued for a distinction between the acts of *Erklären* and *Verstehen*; roughly, explanation (the domain of the natural sciences) and understanding (the domain of the human sciences, where hermeneutical interpretation was held to be appropriate). The distinction between explanation and understanding is not one that can be drawn easily. In English, at least, the two terms are often used more or less interchangeably. However, the distinction is one which highlights a deep fracture in the history of philosophy. Von Wright traces the distinction to the rift between Galilean and Aristotelian approaches to science, which corresponds to the dichotomy between mechanistic and finalistic, or teleological, explanation (von Wright 1971, pp. 1-33).

The Galilean tradition is associated with the European Renaissance and the 'Age of Enlightenment'. In those times intellectual achievements in the natural sciences far outstripped those in the social sciences. However, in the nineteenth century the study of society experienced something of its own renaissance, particularly in Germany, with the first systematic studies in linguistics, philology, social anthropology and historiography (von Wright 1971, pp. 3-7). In the nineteenth century, the relationship between the natural and the social sciences became the subject of intense philosophical debate, with most participants adopting one of two opposing stances.

On the one side was nineteenth-century positivism, exemplified by Comte, and to a lesser extent John Stuart Mill. Nineteenth-century positivists were methodological monists, asserting the methodological unity of all properly scientific work. Their paradigms of scientific method were the exact sciences, particularly mathematical physics. In the tradition of Galileo, they emphasised the importance of laws in explanation and of the causal character of scientific explanation. Nineteenth-century positivists explicitly rejected the Aristotelian category of teleological explanation as unscientific, as have their twentieth-century descendants.

On the other side were a diverse group of thinkers opposed to positivism, who can loosely be called hermeneuticists. Hermeneuticists were disposed towards methodological dualism, accepting, by and large, the positivist treatment of methodology in the natural sciences, but denying the legitimacy of the extension of that methodology to the study of human behaviour. Hermeneuticists emphasise a variety of characteristics of the social sciences that appeared to make them distinct from the natural sciences, (the *Natur-* rather than *Geisteswissenschaften*). The social sciences were said to be idiographic rather than nomothetic; sciences of description, rather than of subsumption under law. They were also set apart in that they were associated with intentionality and reason, dimensions of interpretation said to be absent from the purely natural sciences.

In the twentieth century, an explanation-understanding distinction has been employed, in slightly different forms, by a variety of opponents of positivism and logical empiricism. Principal among these are the 'Frankfurt School', Wittgensteinians such as Peter Winch, and North American 'interpretivists', whom we will consider now. In each case the same basic argumentative strategy has been employed against empiricist explanatory monism: Accept that empiricists have appropriately described explanation in the natural sciences, but deny that that description is applicable to the understanding of human practices.

North American interpretivists of the 1960s and 1970s, such as Taylor and Dreyfus, drew upon the intellectual resources of the hermeneutic tradition, and argued that the then influential positivistic reductive explanatory strategies would not be able to accommodate the richness of human discourse. In marked contrast to the objects of study of the natural sciences, signification and other shared practices that constitute human interaction were described by interpretivists as both holistic and non-essential. We interpret and reinterpret ourselves, and in so doing change what we are.

Stressing both the holistic and anomalous nature of interpretation, interpretivists argue that as interpreters we are caught in a 'hermeneutical circle'. We depend upon the interpretations of others to give meaning to the relations between terms in our shared language. When a dispute arises between ourselves and other interpreters of meaning in our linguistic community, we can only appeal to further, hopefully shared meanings, in order to make our interpretation convincing to them.

Interpretivists hold that, being caught in the 'hermeneutic circle', we must countenance a degree of indeterminacy in our understanding of others. In adopting this stance they contrast their response to the problem of indeterminacy with the responses offered by rationalists and empiricists. Rationalists, such as Hegel, advance the possibility of finding certainty in interpretation, by a process of ascension towards absolute truth via the clarification of reason. Empiricists, on the interpretivist characterisation, advocate breaking out of the hermeneutic circle, by building knowledge on foundations of firm empirical evidence.[2]

The arguments deployed by interpretivists against explanatory monisms are arguments that spring from considerations about the indeterminacy of language use, and would therefore seem to be applicable to the natural sciences as well as to the social sciences. Natural scientists employ language to describe their findings, and to impart information to one another. Methodological dualism is the wrong position to adopt in response to considerations of the indeterminacy of language use. The language used in the natural sciences may be the subject of less controversy than its social science counterparts, but it is certainly not free from considerations of indeterminacy. The natural sciences are subject to the uncertainties of interpretation both in their practice and in the exposition of their results. Nevertheless, we know that particular natural sciences are able to furnish us with highly precise predictions and explanations.

Attempting to pre-empt criticisms along the above lines, interpretivists such as Taylor and Dreyfus insisted that there are methodologically significant differences to be drawn at the natural-science/social-science divide, even if the natural-science/social-science distinction cannot be made as obviously and bluntly as was initially hoped. Taylor (1979) advances three reasons why exacting prediction in the social sciences is 'radically impossible'. He holds that these reasons yield methodologically significant differences between the natural and the social sciences. The three reasons are as follows: First, that we cannot shield areas of human events from external influence. This is known as the 'open systems predicament'. Second, we cannot achieve exactness in the brute data we need to work with. The 'nuances of interpretation' interfere in our attempts to gain precise data about people. Third, and most important, humans are 'self-defining animals'. Changes in our discourse about what we are produce changes in what we actually are, according to Taylor.

Taylor's first argument, that prediction is not possible in the social sciences because of the 'open systems predicament', is a variant of an argument against the possibility of laws of social behaviour, presented earlier by Davidson (1970).[3] On this view, laws of human behaviour are held to be impossible to describe because the possibility of laws of nature depends upon the closure of their subject matter. Unless the subject matter governed by a law of nature is discrete and definable, it will be too open-ended to be governed by exceptionless, universal laws; and the social realm is not one that is closed.

The impact of this argument is lost when one becomes aware of the differences between actual laws, as used by natural scientists, and early positivist views of law-likeness, which did indeed presume closure. The early positivist assumption that laws, in order to be legitimate, must be describable purely within the linguistic resources of one theory or one area of thought — the presumption of closure — was driven by the demands of a thoroughgoing reductionist programme. If one science was to be properly reducible to another, then the resources of the base science would be complete and would 'stand alone'. But this assumption is obviously illegitimate, because its endorsement would rule out almost all of what are currently taken to be laws of natural science. Biochemistry invokes assumptions about chemistry in its description of micro-organisms. Similarly, population genetics makes assumptions about the physical environment in which living organisms compete.

The natural sciences produce successful explanatory and predictive laws despite the 'open systems predicament', and so we can be confident that the inability of the social sciences to achieve closed systems is no barrier to successful nomological explanation and prediction. There may be a genuine insight behind the insistence that the social sciences fail to be predictive because of their openness, which is that it is much more difficult for the social sciences to deal with interfering factors from other disciplines. But the correct conclusion to draw from this insight is not that there is an intrinsic difference between the natural and the social sciences, but that the social sciences are at one end of a continuum of intellectual disciplines in terms of their ability to deal with the interference of external factors when framing explanations.

Taylor's second argument is also defeated by the admission that the natural sciences are interpretive. As in the case of the first argument, we are now faced with a conclusion that is too successful for our own purposes. Being interpretive involves accepting a degree of indeterminacy as a result of the open-endedness of interpretation. However, if being beset by the vagaries of interpretation is a barrier to prediction, then, despite all evidence to the contrary, we will have to conclude that the natural sciences are not predictive: an unacceptable result.

A reformed version of Taylor's third argument is directed at maintaining a natural-science/social-science distinction while conceding that the natural sciences are interpretive. This was presented by Taylor in (1980), where he argued that the distinction between the natural and the social sciences could be maintained despite the interpretive character of the natural sciences, because of the special subject matter of the social sciences. This argument has come to be known as the argument of the 'double hermeneutic'. When scientists study objects which are social, not only are they interpreting, they are interpreting objects that interpret themselves. This consideration has been held by Taylor and others to limit seriously our capacity to secure objectivity in our interpretations.

The third argument, in its reformed guise, is one which sharpens the distinction that Taylor may have been grasping at in his original second and third arguments. Interpretation in the social sciences is distinctive because it is closely connected to our self-understanding. It is here assumed by Taylor that the hermeneutical aspects of inquiry tell us something important about the nature of the objects of inquiry. If our objects of inquiry are themselves inquirers, then, according to Taylor, the nature of our inquiring must alter in some methodologically important way if it is to succeed. In pursuing this line of argument, Taylor argues from a premise about the possibility of our knowledge of a subject to a conclusion about the subject itself. But this is a *non sequitur*. The hermeneutic character of inquiry does not carry a priori implications about the nature of the subject of its inquiry.[4] Indeed, it is difficult to see how it could carry such implications. Hermeneutic argumentative strategies are characteristically holistic and anti-essentialist. As Rouse puts it, 'scientists are obliged to conduct their studies of human beings within such a configuration of meaning, but this requirement says nothing about how human beings will show up as objects within that configuration' (Rouse 1987, p. 173).

3.3 Post-empiricism

As an advocate of epistemic pluralism, I want to deny that the distinction between the subject matter of the human sciences and the natural sciences is any more important than the distinction between the subject matter of different natural sciences, such as physics and biology. Nor is the distinction between the natural and the human sciences more important than that between, say, economics and sociology. There are a variety of ways of knowing the world which have been applied, more or less successfully, in the different scientific disciplines. No one distinction between any of these disciplines is cardinal. In recent times a number of philosophers who can be described as 'post-empiricists' have become increasingly prominent, and are worthy of consideration here because they have argued similarly. Broadly, post-empiricists are writers who attempt to reconcile analytic philosophy with the hermeneutic tradition and develop a synthesis of the two. These post-empiricists include Paul Roth (1987), Joseph Rouse (1987), and James Bohman (1991).

Bohman's *New Philosophy of Social Science* (1991) is a clear and accessible statement of a post-empiricist position. In it Bohman suggests that, rather than attempting to legislate as to what constitutes science, philosophers of science should 'develop critical standards for self-reflection with which to compare various explanatory strategies and patterns' (Bohman 1991, p. viii). This, he says, will help scientists, and people in general, to see knowledge as an 'ongoing social and historical accomplishment' (Bohman 1991, p. viii).

Metaphysics and the Disunity of Scientific Knowledge

It had seemed to empiricist philosophers that in order for science to be set apart from less rigorous human activities, scientific explanations must embody a single implicit ideal of form, against which competing explanations could be compared. Bohman argues that logical empiricist philosophers of science, such as Hempel, have failed to identify this ideal, and that the search for it ought to be given up. His account of this failure of empiricist philosophy of science is heavily indebted to Cartwright. He summarised her arguments against logical empiricist conceptions of explanation as the 'generality-adequacy' problem. On Hempel's D-N account of scientific explanation, an explanation is an argument for which two basic criteria of adequacy must be satisfied. All premises must have assignable truth values and there must be at least one general law. But given Cartwright's account of the ceteris paribus character of laws of nature introduced in Chapter Two, either laws are about fictional objects, or if there are laws true of worldly objects they turn out not to be fundamental laws. They turn out to be laws which are not sufficiently general to uncover powerful explanatory relations between objects in the world. Explanations which fit the D-N pattern can be adequate or general, but not both.[5]

Post-empiricists such as Bohman recognise that problems of interpretation permeate the natural as well as the social sciences. We encounter conditions of indeterminacy in all of the sciences, resulting from the inevitability of human interpretation in scientific practice. The catch-all heading 'indeterminacy' includes several problems which prevent us from accurately determining the exact nature of worldly objects; Quine's indeterminacy of translation thesis, the problem of the theory-ladenness of observation, the Quine-Duhem thesis, and Wittgenstein's problem of rule-following being the central instantiations of indeterminacy discussed in philosophical literature. Unlike postmodern sceptics, post-empiricists do not consider that the interpretive character of all discourse renders scientific knowledge impossible; because, inter alia, they do not consider knowledge to require certainty.

The postmodernist sceptical treatment of indeterminacy, which post-empiricists are opposed to, is embodied in Clifford's (1988) criticism of what is possibly the most widely known recent exemplar of the importance of interpretation: Geertz's (1975) discussion of the Balinese Cockfight. A casual non-Balinese observer at a Balinese cockfight would assume no more than that a sporting event is taking place. However, Geertz argues that a superior interpretation of what is taking place is one which reveals the symbolic importance of the cockfight. Geertz argues that the cockfight is best understood as symbolising class conflict in Balinese society. Clifford and other postmodernist critics attack Geertz for believing that his interpretation of the events at hand is *the* correct interpretation. Geertz writes as if he has put his finger on a truth about the symbolism of the cockfight, an attitude which Clifford criticises him for, insisting that Geertz has constructed rather than discovered the contextual unities needed for his interpretation, such as the assumption of a seamless, coherent Balinese culture in which there are agreed-upon norms of symbolic representation. Clifford and other postmodernists appear to believe that no interpretation of anything is superior to another in any important sense. There is just an unending multiplicity of equally legitimate interpretations, and all that we can legitimately do is catalogue these interpretations.

In criticising authors such as Geertz, postmodernist writers challenge us to explicate our understanding of the art of human interpretation. However, postmodernists err in supposing that the appropriate conclusions to draw from the reality of this challenge are sceptical conclusions. We can admit that we are not certain that Geertz's interpretation is the best possible interpretation of the events surrounding the Balinese cockfight, without being forced to the disastrous conclusion that any interpretation of the events surrounding the cockfight, no matter how ridiculous, is as legitimate as any other. What we can argue, on Geertz's behalf, is that his interpretation appears to be the most plausible interpretation currently available.

3.4 Comparing research programmes

Contemporary epistemic pluralists make much of the tolerance which their position engenders, in marked contrast with the intolerant monistic philosophical characterisations of science and social science of the recent past. Pluralism is suitably tolerant for antifundamentalism when it is tolerant enough to allow that, in principle, there are any number of different methods which could be appropriate to the investigation of different sorts of entities. Any possible method or methods might be most appropriate to a particular science. It should not follow from this that all possible methods are appropriate to any particular science. But, to limit tolerance even to this minimal extent, it looks as if we will need to invoke some common criteria of comparison for competing explanations based on rival methodologies, and this will involve placing some limits on our epistemic tolerance.

Tolerance is a virtue logically related to two vices: intolerance and complacency. If we are too tolerant we run the risk of accommodating too many activities under the heading of science. It is, prima facie, a failing of a philosophy of science if it ends up endorsing such activities as astrology and 'creation science'. An extreme case of complacency occurs when a philosophy of science ends up endorsing unashamedly irrational activities.

The problem facing epistemic pluralism is encapsulated in the career of Paul Feyerabend. In the 1960s Feyerabend was a self-styled pluralist, arguing against logical empiricist presumptions of methodological monism in science. Feyerabend held that we ought to ensure that voices of dissent continue to exist in science, even if this means supporting the practice of particular research programmes that currently offer inferior accounts of known empirical evidence. This is because it is sometimes from the point of view of dissidents that dominant views can best be criticised, and thereby replaced by more progressive ones (Feyerabend 1963, 1965). By the 1970s, Feyerabend's pluralism had broadened to become 'methodological anarchism', the view that there are no methodological standards that should be used to distinguish science from non-science and good science from bad science (Feyerabend 1975). The later Feyerabend endorsed any number of activities alongside science, voodoo being his pet example.

Feyerabend gleefully accepted the irrationalist consequences that followed from his philosophical outlook, with a 'more radical than thou' fervour. Although Feyerabend's position is, so far at least, a lonely one, Feyerabend is problematic for methodological pluralists. His philosophy issues a challenge to the pluralist, which is to find non-arbitrary criteria for refusing to embrace methodological anarchism, once methodological monism is abandoned.

It appears to me that current proponents of pluralism fail to do enough to meet Feyerabend's challenge, to distinguish tolerant pluralism from complacent irrationalism. To highlight this failure I will examine two recent attempts by pluralist philosophers to distinguish their position from irrationalism. I will consider Bohman again, and I then I will consider the work of John Dupré. Unlike many other pluralists, both are sensitive to the threat of irrationalism, but, as I will show, both fail to deal with it adequately.

Bohman's means of avoiding epistemic monism without lurching into anarchism is to argue that we can and do make rational and useful judgements about the success of research programmes without appealing to a common standard to measure that success against. This is done, he maintains, by elucidating standards of success which are internal to particular research programmes, which are then used to make judgements of relative success or failure. To support his claim that such comparisons are rationally possible, he provides a series of examples. We will consider one of his examples of a successful explanatory programme and one of an unsuccessful one.

Ethnomethodology, the sociological research programme associated with Harold Garfinkel, is one example of a research programme which Bohman believes, albeit with some qualifications, is successful. Garfinkel (1967) has pioneered a project of describing social activity in remorseless detail, with the stated aim of revealing the suppositions behind everyday living. Ethnomethodologists see themselves as being opposed to traditional sociologists, such as Garfinkel's mentor Talcott Parsons, who subsume sociological data under ideal models in order to explain them. Ethno-methodologists deliberately eschew such ideal models.

As an example of ethnomethodological research strategy, Bohman cites Garfinkel's series of 'breaching experiments', where the rules and assump-tions of games like tic-tac-toe are deliberately violated in an attempt to expose the ways in which participants in such social practices correct and explain the mistakes of others, so as to make sense of social situations when these threaten to descend into senselessness. Bohman offers qualified approval of ethnomethodological procedure, referring to the ethnomethod-ological programme's '... actual successes in explaining all forms of social order contingently' (Bohman 1991, p. 82). Unlike the ethnomethodologists, however, Bohman does not wish to make a priori assumptions about the impossibility of explanation by appeal to ideal forms. Ethnomethodology is praised by Bohman for showing how '... mutual understanding can be maintained in open-ended practical reasoning ...'(Bohman 1991, p. 99), but criticised because '... the overemphasis on the contexts or settings in ethnomethodology obscures the role that regulative ideals and idealizing suppositions play in rule-governed social action ... ' (Bohman 1991, p. 100).

The Edinburgh-based 'strong programme' in the sociology of science is a research programme that Bohman judges to be a failure. The strong programme distinguished itself from earlier sociologies by refusing to exempt science from sociological analysis. Strong programmers, such as Barnes (1974) and Bloor (1976), believe that the content of scientific knowledge, at a given time, can be explained by appeal to prevailing social conditions as well as the interests of the classes and individuals that are found within those conditions. These conditions are understood to be causal factors subject to the regulation of scientific laws.

Bohman discusses an example of the strong programme methodology, held up by many of the strong programmers as a successful model to guide future work. This is Paul Forman's account of the effect of Weimar culture on the development of quantum theory in 1930s Germany. Forman (1971) attempts to explain the abandoning of traditional notions of causality, by quantum physicists, by appealing to anti-rationalist and anti-scientific tendencies in German culture in the aftermath of World War I. Bohman hangs Forman on the hoist of the 'generality-adequacy' problem. Forman fails to specify the mechanisms by which Weimar culture exerts its influence on the practice of physics. Bohman suspects that this is not done because, if it were to be done, it would either be by specifying very vague mechanisms, which would not apply truly in individual cases, or by supplying a diversity of different specific mechanisms which would not turn out to be similar enough to provide us with explanatory scientific laws. The strong programmers consider science to be practised by specifying scientific laws, and they consider themselves to be scientists. But Forman's study does not specify a single law-like relationship. More generally, the strong programmers fail to specify general laws of the sociology of science, and so fail, in their own terms, to be scientific.[6]

The strong programme in the sociology of science is a highly ambitious enterprise and Bohman is right to conclude that it fails to even approach its own goals. If it is judged dispassionately, against standards implied by it own goals, it must be judged a failure. The project of ethnomethodology, on the other hand, has much more modest ambitions; it aims only at description, avoiding any grand theorising. By its own lights it is a success. So, following Bohman, we could compare the two, judging one a failure and one a success, merely by employing the standards internal to each of the two programmes, thereby avoiding a direct appeal to a common standard of comparison.

What we are doing here, though, is introducing an implicit higher-order common standard of comparison. Each research programme is rated in its own terms and is then cross-rated according to its relative ability to achieve those objectives. Bohman is very pleased with this style of comparison. It lacks the unfashionable look of philosophy sitting in judgement over other disciplines, but still appears to allow us to avoid the charge of irrationalism, by enabling us to rationally compare and criticise research programmes. However, I think that Bohman's methodology manifestly fails to find a pluralist pathway between epistemic monism and anarchism, as the following considerations will show.

Bohman judges the success of research programmes in terms of achievement of articulated goals. Unsurprisingly, this standard will favour the unambitious. The ethnomethodologist aims to do little more than describe, and this seems easily done when compared to the grand ambitions of the strong programmers, who aim to provide law-like scientific explanations of the behaviour of natural scientists, a form of explanation which social scientists have historically failed to provide. But why should we consider that this makes the strong programme a failure when compared to ethnomethodology? This is not how we conventionally judge success. Consider an analogous case involving the comparison of two teenage athletes. Molly wants no more than to win the 100 metre sprint at her school, which she does. Unlike Molly, Polly aims high. She dreams of Olympic gold. She trains hard and is rewarded by selection in her nation's Olympic team. Sadly, on the day of the 100 metre final she is beaten in a three-way photo-finish, and has to be content with a bronze medal. On Bohman's criteria Molly is judged to be more successful than Polly. She has clearly been relatively more successful than Polly at achieving her stated aims. But this is a bizarre conclusion to reach. Conventionally we would say that Polly is the greater achiever of the two. In athletics there is an evident hierarchy against which success is judged. In science and social science the criteria of success are less explicit, but this difficulty in explicating criteria for success does not justify Bohman's inward turn.

Bohman's internal criteria do both too much and too little. The strong programmers have aimed high and have not met their mark; but they do not consider themselves failures. Some of them consider that they have effectively killed off traditional epistemology, and replaced it with the sociology of knowledge, surely a great achievement if true. Bohman's internal criteria do too much; the ability to reach one's own goals is not the only criterion of success. Bohman's internal criteria also do too little. Ethnomethodologists have succeeded in describing social situations in great detail. But this will not appear to be much of an achievement to traditional sociologists. Indeed, as Garfinkel notes, ethnomethodologists do no more than astute observers of life can, such as Agnes, '... a transsexual who so closely observes the details of the production and maintenance of gender identity that her knowledge is equivalent to that gained by the social scientist in documentary observation.'[7] The traditional social scientist wishes to know more about society than the ordinary individual, who is often seen by social scientists as being limited by the framework of her socially influenced ways of understanding. To the traditional social scientist, the suggestion that an observant non-scientist can produce work of similar standard to the social scientist, will look like the admission of failure to go beyond the boundaries of ordinary understanding. Unfortunately, considerations like these cannot enter into Bohman's judgements because they are not internal to the research programmes being considered.

The viability of Bohman's attempt to avoid methodological anarchy depends crucially on his attempt to establish a rational means by which different research programmes can be compared, without employing a common standard of explanation. But this attempt has clearly failed. His examples of rational comparison via comparison of relative success in the light of internal criteria are unconvincing. It is perhaps a good thing that they are unconvincing, because such comparisons are potentially dangerous to the practice of science. Consider if Bohman-style criteria were generally used to allocate funding in the sciences. It would then be in the interests of scientists to aim to achieve very limited goals in order to be judged as successful. Narrow-mindedness and conservatism would reign, attitudes traditionally seen as anathema to the success of science.

3.5 The Disorder of Things

In *The Disorder of Things* (Dupré 1993), John Dupré, our second exemplar pluralist, outlines a philosophy of science that is both metaphysically and methodologically pluralist. Dupré argues against those who hope to see the development of a unified science by painting a detailed picture of the biological sciences which he shows to be rife with disorder. The 'promiscuous realist' account of science he develops as a result is persuasive as a description of the current configuration of these sciences.

Dupré is happy to allow that a diversity of methods characterise the sciences; however, he recognises that there are a number of potential scientific methods advocated by epistemological undesirables which ought not to be characterised as methods befitting the practice of good science. He cites astrology, theology and alchemy, describing these as practices which he holds prejudices against (Dupré 1993, p. 10). He also alerts us to a prejudice against creationism and informs us that it would strike him as '... a fatal flaw in my position if it led to the conclusion that nothing could be said in explanation of the epistemic superiority of the theory of evolution over the apparently competing claims of creationists' (Dupré 1993, p. 242).

Feyerabend's methodological anarchism (Feyerabend 1975) was a distinctive position precisely because of a refusal to cast any methodology as illegitimate. Dupré considers Feyerabend's methodological anarchism and has a seemingly ambivalent attitude towards it. On the one hand he states that '...the philosopher with whose general perspective on science I find myself most closely in agreement, [is] Paul Feyerabend' (Dupré 1993, pp. 262-3). On the other hand he writes that he is reluctant to endorse Feyerabend's extreme epistemic tolerance (Dupré 1993, p. 10). He should indeed be reluctant if doing so would also lead to a 'fatal flaw' in his position; and Feyerabendian epistemic tolerance is characterised by a steadfast opposition to the possibility of the specification of any non-arbitrary criteria which we might use to justify a preference for one methodology over another.

On pain of admission that his position is fatally flawed, Dupré attempts to convince us that evolutionary biology really is an example of good science, whereas 'creation science' is not, by proposing that we should articulate a set of acceptable epistemic virtues. Such a set could then be used to provide grounds to characterise the efforts of creationists as poor science, on the assumption that their practices are shown to be lacking in the requisite virtues. How are we to decide what to include or exclude from our set of acceptable epistemic virtues? According to Dupré we should base our choices on human virtues, which are used to assess scientific methods in terms of 'social worth'. He equates this choice to the evaluation of a science 'in terms of whether it contributes to the thriving of the sentient beings in this universe' (Dupré 1993, p. 264). Epistemic virtues are to be chosen which 'provide an epistemological standard for science that would be overtly and unashamedly normative' (Dupré 1993, p. 243).

It is intuitively obvious that in some communities creationist views would be just the sort of views which would exhibit epistemic virtues accordant with community-given standards of 'social worth', and that in those communities such virtues will make a vital contribution to 'the thriving of the sentient beings in this universe'; when the extent of such contributions to thriving is measured in the terms of those communities. This point hardly warrants an example — but consider a fundamentalist religious community in which the epistemic virtue of revealing divine truths justifies the methodological virtue of literal interpretation of key religious texts. Such a community would be quite likely to favour creationism over evolutionary biology by appeal to such an epistemic virtue, arguing that, when God's truth, as revealed in scripture, is widely disseminated, sentient beings will have better lives. So Dupré has not provided the sort of considerations which could be used generally to portray the creationist as a poor scientist. Epistemic virtues, which are chosen on grounds of social worth, can be used, and almost certainly are used, to justify the methodological superiority of creationism over evolutionary biology.

Presumably, however, Dupré is not concerned to argue that creationists are poor scientists by the lights of any community, only that creationism is justifiably describable as poor science in *our* community. We, then, are a community which is capable of choosing epistemic virtues based on our assessment of social worth, and this choice could justify the categorisation of creationism as poor science. To decide whether we could really justify such a choice, we need to consider who the 'we' are who decide upon epistemic virtues. Either we are a pluralistic community who embrace a variety of epistemic possibilities or we are not such a community. If we are not a pluralistic community then there is no reason to expect that we will choose to support methodological pluralism. We may well choose to support methodological monism, thereby undermining Dupré's position. On the other hand, if we are a pluralistic community which does embrace a variety of epistemic virtues, then we may well have epistemic undesirables in our midst, such as creationists. For example, if 'we' is construed to refer to Western society in general, then we are very obviously members of a pluralistic society in which there is no supreme set of agreed-upon epistemic virtues, and in which minority epistemic virtues, such as the virtue of revelation of divine truth really are sometimes endorsed. We may, of course, choose to exercise our power to force out the epistemically undesirable. But such a choice would be arbitrary. We might equally choose to exclude the evolutionary biologist instead of the creationist. So such a choice would say nothing at all for the *epistemic superiority* of evolutionary biology over creationism. Dupré's stated aim was to show that something could be said '... in explanation of the epistemic superiority of the theory of evolution over the apparently competing claims of creationists' (Dupré 1993, p. 242). But in this he has clearly failed. Therefore, by his own admission, we are entitled to the conclusion that his position, as it stands, is fatally flawed.

We have examined two attempts to construe pluralism in such a way as to distinguish it from irrationalism. Bohman attempted to show that a pluralist philosophy was capable of comparing different research programmes without appeal to a common standard. We saw, however, that his argument was crucially flawed. Dupré attempted to find a basis for the separation of the epistemically respectable from the epistemically disreputable in terms of communal standards. Unfortunately he has not done enough to establish such a criterion of demarcation.

Pluralists need to concede more to Feyerabend than our exemplar pluralists are currently doing. We cannot do without standards of comparison if we are to make comparisons of different research programmes, and we cannot non-arbitrarily exclude those with different standards. I am not going to attempt a full-scale criticism of creation science here, but it seems to me that if one does want to attempt to exclude creation science from science the way to do so is not to look for differences between creation science and mainstream science, but to look for commitments common to both mainstream and creation scientists which will enable comparisons to be made.

Creation scientists have at least this much in common with mainstream scientists: They propound causal explanations of historical events, just as mainstream scientists, such as evolutionary biologists, do. The evolutionist has a historical explanation for the absence of placental mammals in Australia, as does the creation scientist. The usual creation scientist historical explanation for this fact is this: after Noah's ark landed on Mount Ararat the various animals went their separate ways. Fortuitously enough, almost all of the marsupials happened to move across Asia and on to Australia, just before the land-bridge connecting Australia to Asia was severed by rising seas. However, none of the placental mammals managed to get there before the severing of the land-bridge. The creation scientist does not offer evidence from scripture for this historical explanation, but instead means it to be assessed according to the regular standards of acceptance we have for historical explanations. Here then is a point at which creation science and evolution can be directly compared.

Dupré looked for commonality in social values to ground our epistemic choices, and I have argued that this is the wrong place to look because today we live in pluralistic societies in which what is held in common in social values amongst different groups within societies is very little indeed. However, social values are not the only place we can turn to ground our epistemic choices. The next two chapters are an attempt to appeal to causal reasoning as a way of grounding human epistemic values. While values vary considerably between and within communities, what is common among the vast majority of humans is our use of causal reasoning. Therefore an examination of causal attribution is a promising place to look to establish an appropriate restraint on pluralism.

An account of causal attribution will be advanced which will then be related to a theory of the generalisation of causal claims, a theory of idealization. The overall result will be a coherent (albeit somewhat sketchy) view of scientific reasoning as being grounded in and continuous with common-sense causal reasoning.

Notes

---

1   A work that is very clearly an example of this style of argument is Woolgar's *Science: the Very Idea* (1988).
2   See Rabinow and Sullivan (1979), especially the introduction.
3   There are a number of closely related arguments along these lines presented by Davidson, Porpora and Rosenberg. For an intelligent discussion see Kincaid (1990).
4   Okrent (1984) has argued similarly.
5   See Bohman (1991, chapter two, especially p. 26).
6   See Bohman (1991, pp. 40-48).
7   The quotation is from Bohman (1991, p. 79), who paraphrases Garfinkel (1967).

4 Causes and Capacities

4.1 The spirit of Hume

Recall the dilemma that causation presented Hume with, discussed in Chapter Two. Merely contingently true statements are unable to fill the roles that the concept of causal necessity appears to play in causal attribution. However, it looks as if causal claims are contingent truths, at best. Hume places us on the horns of a dilemma. Either we somehow justify belief in the necessity of causal relations, or our conviction that causal attribution is somehow backed by causal necessity is without proper grounds.

Mostly philosophers have opted to grasp the first of these horns, seeing likely sources of causal necessity in concepts such as natural kind, nature, essence, causal law or in causal power. I propose to grasp the second horn of Hume's dilemma, and argue for a non-necessitarian account of causation. I will, following Cartwright, rehabilitate the concept of causal power (which will be referred to as causal capacity), a concept that Hume famously discarded; however, I will do so in a non-necessitarian way. Despite being at odds with the Humean tradition, I see my treatment of causation as very much in the spirit of Hume in that it is unapologetically naturalistic. The naturalistic Hume dispenses with the notion of causal power on the grounds that, if there are causal powers, then these are necessarily detached from our experience. Hume may be right that Locke's and Berkeley's conceptions of causal powers do presuppose the existence of mysterious qualities necessarily beyond our experience. But Hume is wrong to presume that any analysis of causal powers must have this flaw. What I will be concerned to do is to outline a naturalistic capacities-based

73

approach to causation which does not presume that the existence or enduringness of causal capacities is in any sense necessary.

As a pluralist I am suspicious of attempts to understand all uses of a complex group of terms in a straightforwardly unified way. The approach to causation that I will outline is explicitly not intended to account for every last use of causal terminology. Nevertheless, I do intend to advance an account that relates the attribution of enduring causal capacities to objects in the world to the majority of causal claims. I will, following Woodward, show how capacity claims relate to a number of other important types of causal attribution.

My understanding of causation is intended to point the way to a proper characterisation of pluralism that protects it from the sceptical threat posed by philosophical anarchism. What otherwise very diverse humans have in common is concern for the evidence of our senses. A common concern to explain empirical evidence leads us to a shared practice of causal attribution, a shared practice which significantly constrains the possible ways in which we interpret the world. I do not maintain that it is impossible for a person to interpret the world without recourse to causal terminology. However, the vast majority of actual human cultures do practise causal attribution, and do employ causal terms which are structurally homologous to those that are here outlined.[1] It does not and should not worry me that it is possible that some people could interpret the natural world in non-causal terminology. It would concern me, however, if I did not share significant interpretive ground with the majority of people with whom I share a world. The location of a practical-psychological basis for causal attribution is meant to go much of the way towards addressing this concern.

I follow Cartwright in appealing to the existence of enduring capacities to explain the continuing efficacy of causes. In her words:

> If Cs do ever succeed in causing Es (by virtue of being C), it must be because they have the capacity to do so. The capacity is something they can be expected to carry with them from situation to situation (Cartwright 1989, p. 145).

Cartwright is not the only recent philosopher to advocate belief in causal powers or capacities for this purpose. Others to do so include causal realists, such as Harré and Madden (1975), and Bhaskar (1975). However, her position differs substantially from theirs. This difference stems from a difference in motivation. Realists who accept capacities or powers typically do so because they believe that no other justification of the exceptionless character of scientific laws is possible. Cartwright, as I understand her, reverses the commonly accepted relationship between capacities and laws.

Causes and Capacities

Capacities are a useful explanatory concept regardless of whether or not they give us exceptionless laws. In order to be useful for our explanatory purposes, in order to be exportable from one situation to another, capacities must be relatively stable and enduring. The ideal form of relative stability and enduringness is an exceptionless law-like relationship. But we can and do accept the existence of causal capacities on the basis of evidence of considerably less stable and enduring relationships than exceptionless laws.

A complaint that is sometimes laid against Cartwright is that she does not say exactly what it is that capacities are and what they aren't. She does not explicitly define capacities, and nor will I. The commitment that I want to make in committing myself to the existence of capacities is an instance of shallow rather than deep metaphysics. By this, I mean that commitment to the existence of capacities is a commitment to the existence of causally efficacious properties inherent in objects in the world which endure to such an extent that they are reliable for our explanatory purposes. This shallow form of metaphysical commitment is compatible with a variety of deep metaphysical commitments and I see no compelling reason to choose between these.

Recently Woodward has articulated an approach to causal attribution which is much in the spirit of Cartwright. On his view a capacity claim is exportable when it can be shown to be invariant across a wide range of circumstances:

> ... an invariant relationship is a relationship that holds at least roughly or approximately, or in some suitably large number of cases, in the actual circumstances and that would continue to hold in a similar way under some specified class of interventions or for specified changes in background conditions (Woodward 1993, p. 311).

A relationship can be invariant, in Woodward's sense, while being something less than an exceptionless generalisation. Invariance, on his conception, has to do with stability and robustness rather than simple exceptionlessness. Despite having known exceptions, and therefore not being a literally true law, the Ideal Gas Law is an example of the expression of a highly stable and robust relationship between the pressure and temperature of gas, which is explanatorily useful because we know when it will approximate very closely to empirical fact and when it will cease to approximate to the facts. This is not to deny the desirability of literally exceptionless generalisations for explanatory purposes. The standard conception of a law of nature as an exceptionless generalisation represents an ideal to which we would like the relatively stable and enduring invariant generalisations, which we happen to have, to match as closely as possible.

Science is practised by locating invariant patterns in the world and using these as the basis for attributing complexes of causal capacities to particular cases. Armed with knowledge of invariant generalisations, such as the Ideal Gas Law, along with knowledge of the limits of applicability of these generalisations, we are able to perform practical calculations that can be applied to real situations. So, for example, for a large, but not unlimited range of temperatures, we can calculate the pressure at which a given mass of gas would need to be stored were it to be held within a particular container. We make such calculations without the guarantee that there are exceptionless laws of nature.

4.2 Talking causes and capacities

Talk of capacities, powers and the like is endemic to common-sense reasoning as well as to scientific reasoning. It is commonly believed, and scientifically established, that smoking can cause heart disease and that aspirins can cure headaches. When you ask ordinary people what they mean by these claims, they typically reply with words to the effect that there are one or more attributes of the constituents of tobacco which have the enduring capacity to cause hearts to become diseased and that there are one or more attributes of the constituents of aspirin which have the enduring capacity to cause headaches to cease. Scientists will typically express similar views.

Despite the prevalence of the attribution of capacities to entities in common-sense causal reasoning and in scientific reasoning, many philosophers persist in thinking that capacity claims are metaphysically disreputable and somehow mysterious. One way of convincing philosophers that capacity claims are quite mundane is to show that they are well integrated with other forms of causal reasoning. Woodward (1993) distinguishes and relates capacity claims, causal role claims and singular causal claims. We will consider Woodward's work in some detail now, both to show that capacity claims are related to these other sorts of causal claims, and to show how the existence of causal capacities can be established.

On Woodward's account, capacity claims, singular causal claims and causal role claims are logically interrelated in the following ways: It is a sufficient, but not necessary condition for the truth of the claim that events of type C have the capacity to cause events of type E, that an event of type C has caused an event of type E. If a particular token of type C has caused a particular token of type E, then events of type C have the capacity to cause events of type E. For a causal role claim to be true, one or more under-writing causal capacity claims must be true (Woodward 1993, pp. 285-6).

A commonly-used strategy for the establishment of singular causal claims, at the local level, is reasoning by elimination. An event e of type E is observed. We establish that an event c of type C would have the capacity to cause events of Type E. Next we render implausible other possible candidate causes with the capacity to cause events of type E. We do this by drawing up what we take to be a complete list of possible candidates and one by one showing either that they were not instantiated, or that, if they were instantiated, they could not have been instantiated in the right way to be causes of event e.

Woodward's example of this strategy is the Alvarez argument for the mass extinction of the dinosaurs. In their published work the Alvarezes argue that a catastrophic event like the collision of a large asteroid with the Earth could have the capacity to cause the extinction of the dinosaurs via a variety of mechanisms (immediate impact, acid rain fires, etc.). They then argue that other possible mechanisms for extinction of the dinosaurs (e.g. climatic changes) are either inconsistent with the evidence that we have associated with the end of the Cretaceous period, or could not fully account for the extinction of an entire lineage of species.

Causal role claims, such as the claim that smoking was a factor in the increase in the rate of cancer in a population over a given period of time, are typically made with the aid of causal modelling techniques. In this example we aim to establish, not that smoking was solely responsible for the increase in the rate of cancer, nor that smoking was the sole cause of cancer in any particular instance, but that the statistical data we have cannot be explained without recourse to the hypothesis that smoking has played a role in causing an increase in the rate of cancer in the population. All other plausible capacities that we can think of to explain the increase in cancer cannot, without the inclusion of the capacity of smoking to cause cancer, be combined in any way that adequately explains the pattern of cancer which we observe.

It might be thought that causal roles could be established without recourse to capacity claims; that merely with the aid of standard statistical techniques we could establish the existence of causal roles in the absence of considerations about capacities. Woodward argues that in practice this is not how the interpretation of statistical data is conducted. Following

Woodward (1993), let us consider a very simple form of the statistical technique of linear regression. Consider the equation:

$$Y = B_1X_1 + B_2X_2 + \ldots + B_nX_n$$

When we analyse raw data in order to identify covariant relations, such as the relationship between a dependent variable Y and a set of independent variables $X_1 \ldots X_n$, as a matter of practice we make use of a set of coefficients $B_1 \ldots B_n$ to account for the purported interference of other factors in our raw data. Our discretion in altering the coefficient of any variable by adding or deleting other independent variables in these is such that we can expect positive correlation coefficients in a variety of regressions, and so correspondingly expect to support a variety of quite different hypotheses.

In his book *Data Analysis and Policy* (1974), Tufte describes an investigation into the variations in the rate of automobile accidents in the different states of the USA.[2] Tufte regresses a variable measuring automobile fatality rates per state on a number of alternative sets of independent variables: among them, variables measuring whether the state practises regular automobile inspections, its population density, whether it was one of the original thirteen colonies and whether the state has fewer than seven letters in its name. In each case Tufte found a statistically significant, non-zero regression coefficient.

Of course it is intuitively obvious that population density and regular automobile inspection are causally relevant factors, whereas correlations with being one of the original thirteen colonies and having few letters in a state name are either accidental, or they are epiphenomenal correlations, by-products of other genuinely explanatory causal factors. How do we make such judgements? According to Woodward, it is by appeal to implicit knowledge about causal capacities. We know implicitly why low density of population could be expected to lead to greater numbers of accidents — for one thing people in low density areas typically do more driving — and we know implicitly that regular inspections of automobiles have the capacity to prevent accidents, by maintaining high safety standards. In contrast, it is exceedingly hard to imagine how a state's being one of the original thirteen colonies or having few letters in its name could possibly be causally relevant to the rate of automobile accidents.

The view of common-sense and scientific causal reasoning which I have presented, following Woodward, gains support from mainstream contemporary psychological literature on causal attribution, although this is not apparent to psychological researchers writing on causal attribution, who appear to lack an appreciation of the philosophical implications of their own work. The dominant psychological view of causal attribution is the 'covariance' view which is typically presented by its advocates as a variety of Humeanism. The covariance view was proposed by Heider (1958) and developed by Kelley (1973) and others. The idea underlying this approach is that common-sense causal reasoning, as well as causal reasoning in the sciences, is undertaken by making a basic partition between causal factors that are internal and external to an event. The method of partitioning is conducted by looking for enduring covariant relations in a causal sequence across a variety of situations.[3]

Consider the following very simple example. We observe John and Mary dancing gracefully and attempt to determine the cause of their graceful dancing. To do this we invite each of them to dance with a variety of other partners. Suppose that John dances with Ann, Betty and Celia, and we discover that on each occasion the observed dance is more graceful than Ann, Betty and Celia would have had with average dance partners. On the basis of this information, we are inclined to say that gracefulness covaries with the presence of John. If gracefulness covaries with the presence of John and not with the presence of Mary, then we have support for the claim that John's gracefulness was the cause of the graceful dance and that John has the enduring capacity to dance gracefully.

While the covariance view is a fairly accurate depiction of our practices of causal attribution, the psychologists who describe it as a Humean approach are greatly mistaken. What we have done, in the example, is attribute an enduring capacity to an entity, in order to explain why a causal pattern persists. John's enduring capacity for gracefulness was the 'internal cause' of his graceful dance with Mary and it ensures that, ceteris paribus, when he next dances, the dance will be graceful. We have established that John's gracefulness is relatively stable and enduring across a range of circumstances, but not that it is realised in every circumstance without exception. Perhaps John does not exhibit gracefulness in certain circumstances; when he is under hypnosis, or receiving certain forms of medication, for example. For a Humean-style view of causal attribution, one which directed us to find regularities across an unqualified domain, these considerations would militate against the conclusion that John is a graceful dancer. But, because we attribute capacities to objects and people across a limited (invariant in Woodward's sense) range of useful cases, these considerations are not relevant to the question of whether or not John has the capacity for graceful dancing.

4.3 Manipulation, enduringness, stability and autonomy

As we saw in Chapter Two, Cartwright holds that causal capacities are attributable to entities because of our ability to manipulate those entities and intervene in their activity. Similar views have been advocated by Hacking (1983), von Wright (1971) and Gasking (1955). Our ability to manipulate items and intervene in their activity gives us access to important sources of information, which can enable us to conclude that stable and enduring causal capacities are carried by those items. A discussion of Gasking's work (Gasking 1955) will help to clarify this point.

Gasking invites us to consider the case of a very hot iron bar which is glowing brightly. The temperature of the bar and its glow are simultaneous with one another. On a standard Humean approach to causation we cannot say that the heat causes the glow or that the glow causes the heat, as neither occurs prior to the other. However, ordinary usage allows us to say, authoritatively, that the heat of the bar causes its glowing and it definitely does not allow us to say that the glowing of the bar causes its heat.

Gasking suggests the following explanation of the asymmetry of our attribution of causal terms in the iron bar case. We say that the iron bar's heat causes its glow, and not vice versa, because (typically) the way in which the iron came to be hot and glowing involved our manipulation of the bar's temperature rather than its radiance. We heated the iron bar and thereby made it glow. Manipulability is ordinarily associated with temporal order. Usually, when we manipulate an item, the effects that follow our intervention in its activity are subsequent to that intervention. The prevalence of the usual situation has perhaps misled philosophers into thinking that temporal order is a necessary mark of a causal sequence. However, the general case of a causal relation, for Gasking, is one where we are able to manipulate an item and cause its behaviour, or that of other items affected by it, to alter. Many of these cases are ones in which a cause precedes its effect. Nevertheless, an event can properly be said to be a cause of a simultaneous event when our intervention in the activity of one affects the other.

Gasking is right to point to manipulability as a criterion for causal attribution. However, he seems to believe that causation is merely manipulability.[4] As it stands, this view is strongly counterintuitive. We unproblematically attribute causal relations to sequences of events in which humans are involved only as passive observers rather than as manipulators. Furthermore, we attribute causal relations to sequences of events which we do not intervene in, and are not likely to be able to intervene in. For example, we believe that nuclear fusion causes the sun to shine, and we believe this without having the ability to intervene in the process of nuclear fusion within the sun.

A capacities-based account of causation makes good sense of the importance of manipulability in causal attribution. Manipulability is important to the epistemology of causation because it allows us to individuate causal capacities. Very often we are presented with a mix of causal capacities. It is by exhaustively manipulating such mixtures that we are able to identify their causal constituents. The sense in which there can be simultaneity of cause and effect is accounted for by the possibility of an object or its properties carrying multiple capacities. So pieces of iron carry the dual capacities to cause heat and radiance. We happen to be able to manipulate one of these capacities directly, and the other indirectly through the first. As a matter of convenience in such cases, we refer to the former capacity as cause and the latter as effect.

We have spoken of stability and enduringness as being important qualities of invariant causal capacities. We can say more about these qualities once we appreciate the role of manipulability in the epistemology of causal capacities. A stable and enduring relationship is one that is highly autonomous across a wide range of transformations. The importance of autonomy for useful causal attribution has long been recognised in the field of econometrics. In a well-known example, Haavelmo (1944) asks us to consider the exercise of testing the relationship between the pressure applied by a driver's foot to the throttle of a car, and the corresponding speed of the car, in a series of tests on a flat dry road.[5] Although we might reasonably expect to be able to describe a mathematically exact relationship between the two variables, if we know much about driving contemporary cars in contemporary road conditions we would consider the exercise a poor use of our time. This is because the relationship between the two variables which we describe lacks autonomy. Given even a small alteration in the internal mechanisms of the car, or in the quality of the road surface, we can expect the actual relationship which we found between the pressure on the throttle and the speed of the car to deviate dramatically from that which we found under experimental conditions.

The standards of autonomy which we endorse are pragmatic ones. If we lived in a world where cars rarely broke down and roads were reliably flat and dry, then a nomic relationship between throttle depression and car speed would be autonomous in that world. However, even in such a world we would hesitate to call such a relationship invariant. Invariance suggests counterfactual considerations as well as actual ones. A properly invariant relationship ought to hold under a variety of transformations of circumstances, factual and counterfactual; which is to say that it ought to be robust. Like the case of the reliable car in the hypothetical world of uniformly flat dry roads, some actual reliable generalisations lack the quality of robustness. We will consider the concept of robustness in the next section, in the context of a discussion of the interrelation of causal and counterfactual claims.

4.4 Capacities and causal counterfactual claims

Causal attributions generate counterfactual claims. Because, following Woodward, I invoke considerations of robustness in explicating the concept of invariance, and because robustness is a concept with counterfactual import, it will be helpful to explain how causal counterfactual claims are generated, on my approach. When I claim that an aspirin has the capacity to relieve headaches, I appear to imply that, if someone with a headache had taken an aspirin, then, ceteris paribus, their headache would have been relieved.[6]

A useful resource for me is the explication of the evaluation of sequential counterfactuals in terms of causal laws, due to Frank Jackson (1977). Jackson provides an informal description of his approach:

> The causal laws of the actual world determine for each physically possible state of the world at a time, the state of the world at all subsequent times. Take the state of the world at the antecedent-time, change it as little as possible in particular facts, while still making the antecedent true, and keep earlier facts just as they are. Then consider whether, operating on the minimally changed time-slice, the causal laws of the actual world predict subsequent states which make the consequent true (Jackson 1977, pp. 9-10).

At first glance it might appear that Jackson's causal account of sequential counterfactuals is of little help to me because it analyses these in terms of causal laws, and I wish to avoid commitment to an ontology of causal laws. I do not, however, simply *disown* causal laws. I hold that they are idealizations; playing a crucial role in our explanations of the world, although this is rarely if ever the role of representing the world as it truly is. Counterfactual conditionals that are derived from universal causal generalisations are similarly idealizational. We typically intuit a range of counterfactual claims to be true when we have established an invariant causal generalisation. So we can put Jackson's approach to sequential counterfactuals to work with a few suitable modifications: The causal laws of a chosen robust, invariant, idealization from facts about the actual world determine, for each physically possible state of that idealized world at a time, the state of that idealized world at subsequent times. Take the state of the idealized world at the antecedent time, change it as little as possible in particular facts, while still making the antecedent true, and keeping earlier facts just as they are. Then consider whether, operating on the minimally changed time-slice, the causal laws idealized from the actual world predict subsequent states which make the consequent true.

So, for example, the Ideal Gas Law $pV=nRT$ is an idealization of facts from the actual world, which describes an invariant relationship between the pressure, volume and temperature of gases. Suppose we want to decide whether we are going to assent to the counterfactual claim that if we had increased the pressure of a sample of gas in a balloon, G, the temperature of that gas would have risen. Consider the idealized world where the behaviour of gasses is governed by the Ideal Gas Law, and consider a sample of gas, G_I, at the same temperature, pressure and volume as G. Now change the facts of the idealized world to make it true that the pressure of the sample of gas G_I is greater, and then consider what the Ideal Gas Law would predict of G_I. It would, of course, predict that if we raised the pressure on G_I, the temperature of the gas would also rise. So we are entitled to assent to our idealized counterfactual.

Non-idealized capacity claims can be tested against counterfactual intuitions, which can be used to investigate the robustness of causal attributions. We invoke intuitions about counterfactual conditionals when, following Woodward, we ask ourselves whether our causal attributions continue to hold when initial and background conditions are transformed in various ways. Exactly which transformations of initial and background conditions are relevant to the testing of causal generalisations? Our choice of salient counterfactual tests of a capacity claim will depend upon relevant background beliefs about other causal capacities in this world. It is a result of my background beliefs about genetics and pigmentation that I believe that the true generalisation 'all ravens are black', although autonomous in relation to other causal factors of this world, is not particularly robust. It is not hard to conceive of there being non-black ravens to be found in worlds which are similar to this one, and perhaps in the future time-slices of this world. Consider, however, the true generalisation 'all ravens have hearts'. This generalisation is highly robust, the reason being that we believe it would be a very extreme and unlikely mutation of a raven's offspring that both removed or replaced its heart and enabled it to continue existing.

Again, our knowledge of the limitations of possible transformations of entities in this world is pertinent.

Causal relations are typically attributed to the world as a result of the identification of invariant relations, which are then idealized to yield causal laws; and idealized causal laws support counterfactual claims, making causal generalisations intuitively seem necessary to us. Hume provided part of the explanation of our intuition that causal relations are necessary when he showed us that sheer force of habit leads us to assume that causal relations are necessary. But there is more to be said by way of explanation of the pervasiveness of the presumption that causal relations are necessary ones. The utility of idealized laws in explanation is an additional source of our sense that causal relations involve some sort of necessary connection.

4.5 Experimental science and irregular capacities

An ontology of causal capacities can help explain why knowledge gained via experiments performed in highly artificial laboratory conditions is exportable to non-laboratory situations, which may be very different from those laboratory situations. It is the invariance of certain capacities that enables information about those capacities, discovered in the laboratory, to be usefully reapplied in complex worldly conditions. The possibility of the experimental sciences being successful is predicated on the assumption that causal capacities discovered in laboratories are strongly invariant. Weakly invariant capacities, ones which are lacking in stability and robustness, will not do for reliable exportation from simple laboratory situations to complex worldly ones.

Cartwright's work focuses mainly on the laboratory sciences, while Woodward has focused on the social sciences. This difference in emphasis has led to a key difference in their respective positions. Cartwright argues that capacities need to satisfy what Dupré (1993) refers to as a 'contextual unanimity requirement', a condition of acceptability often invoked in work on probabilistic causation. Cartwright expresses the contextual unanimity requirement as 'Principle CC':

> Principle CC: 'C causes E' if and only if the probability of E is greater with C than without C in every causally homogeneous background (Cartwright 1989, p. 142).

Such a requirement is too stringent, according to Woodward. He argues that capacities need only be relatively invariant, and that invariance is compatible with a significant degree of non-uniformity or irregularity in the behaviour of causal capacities (Woodward 93, p. 1).[7]

Much of the detail of Cartwright's argument for capacities is concerned with problems of statistical explanation. She argues that realists about probabilistic causation such as Salmon, Eells and Sober employ a notion of cause that implicitly presupposes the existence of causal capacities. They typically do this by invoking some form of contextual unanimity requirement, which Cartwright (1989) argues is only justifiable if the existence of enduring capacities is implicitly presumed. Cartwright is right to argue that these writers do implicitly commit themselves to contextual unanimity when dealing with probabilistic causation, and so are implicitly committed to capacities. Unfortunately this line of reasoning motivates her to unconditionally insist upon a contextual unanimity requirement herself, when considering statistical explanation. In practice, scientists do not require anything as stringent as the satisfaction of a contextual unanimity requirement to accept the existence of causal capacities. To see this we need only consider the stock example of the probabilistic causation literature, 'smoking causes heart disease in humans'. If we accept that the capacity of smoking to cause heart disease in humans satisfies a contextual unanimity condition, then we are committed to holding that smoking always increases the probability that a given human will contract a heart disease, in spite of an almost inexhaustible list of other properties which humans might also happen to have, that could conceivably affect the rate at which heart disease is contracted. We would then be committing ourselves to holding either that smoking has the propensity to cause an increase in the chance of getting heart disease, regardless of a person's race, gender, political outlook or taste in music etc., or retracting our claim that smoking causes heart disease.

Scientists have not established that the act of smoking always increases the propensity of all humans to have heart disease, and it would not be surprising to discover that some humans, due to particular cultural circumstances, or perhaps due to genetic peculiarities, fail to suffer from an increase in their propensity to experience heart disease when they smoke. Such considerations need not lead us to doubt the validity of causal claims, such as the claim that smoking causes an increase in the rate of heart disease among humans. Instead we can allow that smoking has an *irregular* capacity to cause heart disease.

What exactly is an irregular capacity? Just as a capacity might be irreducibly statistical in nature, it might also be irreducibly irregular. Cs might have an enduring capacity to produce Es, but might actually do so in a way that was unpatterned, and hence not properly describable as a statistical relationship. If a relationship between Cs and Es were irregular it would be true that in x% of actual cases Cs caused Es, but untrue that Cs had a propensity to produce Es in x% of cases. If Cs have the capacity to produce Es, what is important for 'capacityhood' is that Es continue to be produced in the presence of Cs across a range of different circumstances more frequently than in the absence of Cs, regardless of whether there is a completely regular relationship to be found between Cs and Es.

Despite the lack of evidence for a nomic probabilistic relationship between smoking and heart disease, scientists confidently assert that smoking causes heart disease. They do this while knowing that the correlation between smoking and heart disease varies considerably as other factors (e.g. gender, socio-economic class, nationality, etc.) are varied. What we do consistently find is, first, that the rate of heart disease is higher among those who smoke than those who don't, across a broad domain of circumstances, and, second, that within this broad domain heavy smokers almost always have a greater rate of contraction of heart disease than light smokers. In the face of this sort of evidence scientists take the hypothesis of rival explanations for the statistical relationship between smoking and heart disease to be implausible, despite not having themselves established a regular statistical relationship between smoking and heart disease.

Woodward (1993) makes what I take to be a strong case for accepting irregular capacities. In doing so he appears to be seriously at odds with Cartwright, whose account of capacity-based explanations requires that capacities satisfy a unanimity requirement, and therefore that they be regular in at least this one sense. I side with Woodward here. However, I think that there is something to be said in defence of the motivations which have led Cartwright to ignore the possibility of irregular capacities.

Woodward has been concerned with the ascription of capacities in cases where capacities are manifested as singular causes or as causal role claims. In these cases, we don't need to have a precise measure of a capacity's propensity to be manifested in order to provide satisfactory explanations. In the case of singular causation, we proceed by showing that a particular capacity C which could produce an effect of type E is present, and all other candidate capacities that could produce an effect of type E aren't present. In the case of causal role claims, we proceed by establishing that a particular capacity C is present, and that the combination of other capacities which may be present is not sufficient to explain the incidence of E. In neither case do we have to know the exact measure of the propensity of Cs to cause Es, so Cs that we can discover which do not have regular propensities to produce Es are acceptable for our purposes.

Cartwright focuses on a different explanatory task. She is concerned principally with exportation: with cases where we find a capacity in a simple situation and then attempt to export that knowledge to complex situations. If we want to establish that a particular capacity is present in a complex situation where there are sufficient other potential causal factors present to produce an explanation, we will need to have more exact information about that capacity. We will need to be able to measure the expression of a capacity, and to be confident that our measurement will reliably inform us as to how it will operate in different situations. The more irregular the capacity, the less reliably we will be able to export information about it. Common-sense causal reasoning is centrally involved with the attribution of enduring capacities in the world. There is no one way in which this is done. Occasionally capacities throw up regularities in the world for us to quantify. Often however, given the complexity of our world, we have to manipulate objects and intervene in causal processes, in order to uncover covarying patterns in the world indicative of the existence of invariant capacities.

Appreciating this much, we are in a position to outline a two-stage general theory of scientific practice. When the practice of a particular scientific discipline is in its infancy, that discipline amounts to no more than the rigorous application of the processes of common-sense causal reasoning in a particular area of study. However, common-sense causal reasoning cannot be more than merely approximate. In order for a discipline to progress to a stage where it can be used to put forward powerful explanatory and predictive theories, it needs to be transformed into a discipline of precise measurement. Only then can the relative contributions of different causal factors to a particular effect be determined. The most successful scientific disciplines are the laboratory sciences. In the laboratory particular causal processes can be isolated and precisely measured. Non-laboratory sciences, principally the biological and the social sciences, are sciences that depend on statistical techniques to make up for their practitioners' relative inability to manipulate and intervene in a controlled situation, and they have so far failed to attain the accuracy needed to transcend this boundary. In the next chapter I outline a theory of idealization. This will show how the experimental sciences can and do transcend the limits of common-sense causal attribution, to produce powerful explanatory theories. It is by idealizing that we are able to transform information gained in the laboratory into precise exportable data about the magnitude of causal capacities.

Notes

1   The work of Robin Horton (1993) appears to be addressed at substantiating just this claim in the case of African cultures.
2   Discussed in Woodward (1993, pp. 297-8).
3   Hilton (1988) outlines the development of the covariance view. A more comprehensive review of contemporary psychological literature on causal attribution is to be found in Cheng and Novick (1992).
4   Although he qualifies this bald formulation of causation in concluding his discussion (Gasking 1955, p. 487).
5   The example is discussed in Woodward (1995, pp. 11-3).
6   The aim of this section is to suggest how counterfactual considerations are psychologically generated by the acceptance of capacity claims. I specifically do not wish to be understood to be attempting to provide the basis for a logical analysis of counterfactual conditionals.
7   Bigelow and Pargetter also argue against the equivalent of a contextual unanimity condition in probabilistic causal attribution, which they refer to as the assumption of 'probability boosting' (1990, pp. 270-5).

5 Idealization

5.1 An idealizational approach to science

Scientific reasoning does not initially differ from common-sense causal reasoning, which is directed, *inter alia*, at the attribution of relatively stable and enduring capacities to objects. However, there are inherent limitations to such reasoning. While the capacity claims of common-sense reasoning are exportable, they are not suitable for redeployment in the explanation of complex situations in anything more than a rough and ready way. To provide explanations with the potential for predictive accuracy in complex situations we need to be able to measure, very precisely, the magnitudes of invariant causal capacities.

The laboratory sciences are disciplines in which causal capacities have been successfully isolated and redeployed with explanatory and predictive success in complex worldly situations.[1] A plausible depiction of science should be able to account for the ability of the laboratory sciences to provide explanations which are generalisable and applicable outside of the context of laboratories. Cartwright, when faced with the related problem of accounting for the explanatory power of ideal fundamental laws in worldly situations, turned to the work of Leszek Nowak. Nowak (1980) has developed a reconstruction of Marx's *Das Kapital*, which he generalises as an idealizational theory of science. Cartwright describes Nowak's account of the transformation of abstract laws into concrete ones as 'the most detailed work on abstraction' and as '[seeming] right in its basic outline' (Cartwright 1989, p. 202).

In this chapter I introduce the topic of idealization in its historical context. Then, I examine Nowak's account of idealization and consider some of the more important objections that might be raised against it. In the process of considering these objections I will refine Nowak's account of idealization in such a way as to integrate it with the treatment of causation presented in the previous chapter. Additionally I outline a treatment of scientific progress which is sensitive to the idealizational character of scientific explanation.

5.2 The two dialogues

The view that the fundamental laws of science are idealizational is a view that is opposed to the dominant empiricist traditions of the twentieth century. However, if we consider a broader sweep of intellectual history, we find that the idealizational view is one that is deeply rooted in modern European scientific thought. More than this, it is seminal to that thought, being the methodological key to the overthrow of Aristotelianism which took place in the Renaissance. It is expressed most clearly in Galileo's anti-Aristotelian polemics.

Galileo's name is often identified with the rise to prominence of laws of nature in the practice of science. However, Galileo did not view laws Humean-style, as regularities of sensory data. Koyré makes clear that Galileo, far from anticipating recent empiricist thinking — as a number of positivist-influenced philosophers of science have alleged — was opposed to the Aristotelianism of his day on the matter of its insistence on the immediate importance of sensory data in scientific explanation.[2] Galileo's opposition to radical empiricist attitudes is strongly suggested by the following passage from the *Dialogue Concerning the Two Chief World Systems*:

> ... there is no limit to my astonishment when I reflect that Aristarchus and Copernicus were able to make reason so conquer sense that, in defiance of the latter, the former became mistress of their belief (Galilei 1953, p. 328).

These are not the words of a Humean-style empiricist. Galileo believed that the process of interpreting sense-data properly involves their selective use, and that a knowledge of how to interpret sense-data selectively is what is lacking among his adversaries. But which particular possible selective use of sense-data did Galileo advocate? And why would any particular selective use of data be justifiable? The *Dialogue Concerning the Two Chief World Systems* contains his answer to these questions. The dialogue is between Simplicio, representing the Aristotelian tradition, Salviati, the spokesman

Idealization

for Galileo's reasoning, and Sagredo, an initially open-minded participant who is won over to Salviati's side by the force of his arguments. Salviati's argumentative strategy is aimed at justifying the use of geometry as the 'language of physics', so as to show that, contrary to Aristotle (as he was understood at the time), it is legitimate to utilise ideal cases to inform thought about real cases. The actual attitude of Aristotle towards idealizational explanation is a complex question, but it is not a question that we need be directly concerned with. Scepticism about the application of strictly ideal mathematical concepts to real situations was the predominant attitude amongst the Aristotelians of Galileo's era (McMullin 1985, p. 250).

Against Salviati's application of mathematical abstraction to the material realm Simplicio objects:

> After all, Salviati, these mathematical subtleties do very well in the abstract, but they do not work out when applied to sensible and physical matters. For instance, mathematicians may prove well enough in theory that a sphere touches a plane at a single point, ... but when it comes to matter, things happen otherwise. What I mean about these angles of contact and ratios is that they all go by the board for material and sensible things (Galilei 1953, p. 203).

Salviati responds to this objection by drawing an analogy between the 'geometrical philosopher' and a merchant, who must allow for the weight of packaging materials when he calculates the actual weight of his wares. He argues that the discrepancies between the physical world and the hypothetical world of perfect geometric solids that it approximates to, can also be accounted for by making such allowances:

> ... when he wants to recognise in the concrete the effects which he has proved in the abstract, [he] must deduct the material hindrances, and if he is able to do so, I assure you that things are in no less agreement than arithmetical computations. The errors, then, lie not in the abstractness or concreteness, not in geometry or physics, but in a calculator who does not know how to make a true accounting (Galilei 1953, pp. 207-8).

We can legitimately explain the behaviour of real objects by appealing to the theoretical behaviour of ideal objects when we are able to justify the use of the corrections needed to reproduce accurate representations of real situations using ideal ones. We can do this if we can accurately calculate the contribution that interfering causes make in a particular situation. To explain why the weight of the merchant's wares is what it is, we subtract the assessed weight of the packaging from the total weight, arriving at an idealized weight for those wares, in the absence of the interfering effect of the packaging on their weight. Our ability to justify our chosen corrections tests the correctness of our idealizations.

Recent empiricist philosophers of science clearly have not understood laws of nature as being idealizational. If the Galilean revolution in scientific methodology was centred upon the rejection of Aristotelian qualms about the use of idealized laws, then it is stunning that among the mid-twentieth-century empiricist heirs of the Galilean revolution, not only have fundamental explanatory laws of nature not been held to be characteristically idealizational, but also the question of the idealness of laws has not even been much debated.

In part this recent attitude is due to a widespread policy, among mid-twentieth-century empiricist philosophers, of ignoring details of the practice of science, in favour of 'rational reconstruction', on the grounds that such details are potentially obfuscatory. In part it may also be explained by the uses which opponents of empiricism have sought to make of the idealizational nature of laws of science. In the nineteenth and early twentieth centuries, neo-Kantians and conventionalists did emphasise the idealness of laws of nature — in the case of neo-Kantians, to stress the supposedly a priori nature of scientific thinking, and in the case of conventionalists to further relativist conclusions. Galileo's intellectual heritage became divorced from discussion of idealization in such an intellectual climate. Perhaps though, the most tangible reason for the lack of attention paid to idealization by twentieth-century empiricists is that leading figures among them believed that they possessed an account of the actual usage of idealizational laws by scientists, which enabled them to dismiss the subject as unimportant: a topic which we discussed in Chapter Two.

Humean empiricists have typically seen the scientific revolution as a purge, in which the metaphysical elements present in Aristotelian science were evicted to make way for a methodology that started and ended with things empirical. They understand the rounding up and expelling of stray metaphysical concepts that have taken refuge in the guise of empirical concepts to be the chief responsibility of philosophers of science.[3] I see the project of metaphysical auditing as a philosopher's venture which has been read into the history of science by Humean empiricist philosophers.

Cartwright also disagrees with the Humean empiricist version of the history of science. On Cartwright's (1992) view, Humeans err in conceiving of the scientific revolution as a banishing of occult talk of natures in favour of the measurement of empirical regularities. She understands the philosophically decisive move characterising the scientific revolution to be a deformation of Aristotelian natures (which were occult powers, essentially hidden from us), turning them into powers or natures or capacities that are to be found at the 'surface of nature' where we can observe them — mostly in those places which scientists locate in experiments (Cartwright 1992, pp. 46-7).

While Cartwright is right to challenge the empiricist orthodoxy her own view of the history of science is somewhat one-sided and stands in need of supplementation. As Kuhn argues, there are two transformations that jointly constitute what we now call the 'scientific revolution'. The first is the move to idealization identified with Galileo, and the second is the emphasis on experimentation which arose independently, and is associated with Bacon, Gilbert, Harvey and other, mostly British, empirical scientists (Kuhn 1977, pp. 31-65). I take it that Cartwright would accept the importance of the recognition of the legitimacy of idealizational reasoning in a charaterisation of the scientific revolution. Cartwright endorses idealizational reasoning and it is Galileo's advocacy of idealizational explanations which has enabled appeals to causal capacities identified in laboratories to be explanatorily relevant outside of the narrow confines of those laboratories.

A depiction of the scientific revolution that accords with the views of the most thorough historians of science of recent times will be one which requires two things: first, a decisive move away from an insistence on the 'normal case', which was reified by medieval Aristotelians, and, second, a move to a conviction that one could discover enduring causal capacities by a process of devolving real situations and studying them at their 'causal seams'; the method of idealization.[4] Natures do survive the scientific revolution, as Cartwright and I, but not mainstream Humean empiricists, think they do. However, they do so in a form that is neither 'at the empirical surface', as Cartwright (1992) holds, nor as typical specimens of an essential natural kind, as an Aristotelian might believe.

5.3 Idealization and concretization

The most thorough contemporary work on idealization has come from the Poznan school: a group of Polish philosophers who have been committed to the project of bringing the clarity of analytic philosophy to Marxist thought. Nowak is the most prolific and the most influential member of the school. His work has found its way from Poland into the English-speaking world in various places. Its most complete expression can be found in his *The Structure of Idealization* (1980). Nowak (1980) is an outline of an original philosophy of science developed in order to defend an interpretation of

Marx's *Das Kapital.* Nowak holds that Marx (1968a) is a scientific work, that identifies *the* correct scientific method, which is common to both the natural and the social sciences, and applies it in the field of political economy. In contrast to other Marxists, who make similar claims on behalf of Marx, Nowak is sensitive to the detail of actual scientific practice and aware of the main currents to be discerned in recent western philosophy of science. Nowak's methodology is Galilean. He holds the method of idealization to be the key feature which distinguishes scientific from pre-scientific thinking. His defence of a scientific Marx amounts to the claim that Marx is 'the Galileo of the social sciences' (Nowak 1980, p. 38).

Like Galileo, Nowak's Marx is a thinker who finds himself in an intellectual atmosphere of dogmatic insistence on the importance of the empirical. In this context he is a pioneer in the development of a social science that is concerned to look 'beneath the surface' of social phenomena. We will not here be concerned with defending Nowak's interpretation of Marx, although we will be concerned with Nowak's use of Marx as an exemplar of idealizational methodology in the social sciences.[5]Nowak sees scientific reasoning as characteristically involving the systematic employment of idealizing assumptions in order to 'lay bare' the magnitudes of the different causal factors that make up complex worldly situations. His philosophy of science is explicitly a development of Galileo's technique of mathematical abstraction and is a close relative of Mill's methods of experimental inquiry.

Galileo may have been a prime instigator of the scientific revolution, but examination of his works reveals that he paid scant attention to the confirmation of scientific hypotheses. In particular, Galileo paid little attention to precise experimental control and repetition, which are accepted as part of normal scientific practice today. Recognising the deficiencies in Galileo's work, the Galileans of the Poznan school develop his ideas in two ways. First, they devote considerable emphasis to the process of concretization, the process by which idealizational laws can be related to real situations and thereby confirmed or falsified. Second, they attempt to formalise the processes of idealization and concretization, to show that their account of scientific methodology is itself scientific in its precision.

The terms 'idealization' and 'abstraction' are closely related, but are usually intended to refer to different processes. I think that the following captures the distinction well enough for our purposes: Abstraction is the omission of properties of individuals in order to form sets of objects. Red, blue and green billiard balls all have the same counterpart, devoid of colour, in the abstract set of colourless spheres. Idealization is the substitution of some properties in order to render others irrelevant. When accounting for the trajectories of interacting billiard balls we typically idealize to the assumption that all balls being considered are perfect spheres. This transformation may involve the subtraction and addition of many properties in particular cases as individual real billiard balls are mentally transformed into perfect spheres. In practice idealization will typically involve some abstraction — perfect spheres are usually considered to be colourless and lacking in other irrelevant properties. Typically such irrelevant properties are causally inert. We need to understand which properties are causally inert, and therefore abstractable, and which are causally relevant when we idealize.[6]

The processes of concretization and idealization are reflections of one another. Idealization is the process of subtracting the influence of interfering causes from a situation in order to determine what effects the causal agent we are focusing on is causing, and concretization is the process of adding these back in. In Nowak's terminology, the object of our study is a 'primary factor'. The sources of causes that interfere with the expression of the primary factor in a particular situation are 'secondary factors'. We idealize by working through what we take to be a complete list of secondary factors, and making appropriate adjustments to empirical facts to determine the outcome that the primary factor would have caused if it had not been interfered with by secondary factors. We concretize by considering other situations in which we have reason to believe that our primary factor is causally efficacious, and modifying that result by amounts appropriate to the particular levels of influence of secondary factors that we believe to be present in those situations. If we attain the results in practice that we have calculated, then we have a confirming instance of the presence of our primary factor. If we fail to attain those results then, *prima facie*, we have a falsifying instance.

There have been several attempts by members of the Poznan school to formally describe the processes of idealization and concretization. I will present a slightly modified version of Krajewski's (1977) formalisation.[7] Ideal objects differ from real objects in having properties of convenience, properties constructed so that the parameters that will affect our equations can be ascribed a convenient value. Nowak assumes that the only value of convenience in the process of idealization is zero, although he fails to argue for this exclusivity. Generally, x is an ideal object when it is an ideal limit of a series of possible real objects which are alike in that they have a series of values of a parameter that asymptotically approach some value of convenience — henceforth assumed to be zero. An obvious example of an ideal object is a frictionless plane. This can be understood to be an ideal limit of a series of real planes ordered according to their capacity to cause successively less and less friction.

An ideal law can be related to empirical reality with a set of idealizing assumptions. Nowak presents an idealizational exposition of Marx's law of value as an example of this form of relation. For Marx the law of value relates the price of commodities to the total amount of labour time involved in the production of those commodities. Nowak (1980) argues that Marx's law of value should be understood as a highly idealized law, literally true only when a number of potential interfering factors, which ordinarily do interfere in real situations, happen not to interfere. He identifies eight such idealizing assumptions, which must all be satisfied for the systematic application of Marx's law of value to empirical reality.

So, for example, the law of value is not strictly true of a given economy when the value of imports into the economy differs from the value of exports leaving the economy. In such cases, price will not equate to value. But imports and exports are not ordinarily balanced. An explicitly formulated idealizing assumption would enable a Marxian economist to calculate the exact magnitude of the distortion in the price of a commodity from its true value due to the discrepancy between imports into, and exports out of, an economy where that commodity is produced.

The eight idealizations in Nowak's exposition of Marx's law of value are each designed to reduce to zero the value of a parameter (p) that represents the effect of an interfering factor on an ideal object (x). In this case (x) is a particular commodity and we are attempting to determine its true value. Each idealizational stage in the series accounts for one such factor and has the general form

$p_n(x) = 0.$

So, for example, the law of value is used with the idealizing assumption already discussed: that exports (E) and imports (I) are in exact balance, which will be true when the second of the eight idealizing assumptions is true:

$p_2[I(x) - E(x)] = 0.$

Another example from the same idealizational series is an idealizing assumption motivated by the recognition that differences between the demand for a product and supply of that product can distort the price of that product away from its true value. The seventh idealizing assumption is that demand (D) exactly equals supply (S), and this can be formalised as

$$p_7[D(x) - S(x)] = 0.$$

A complete set of idealizing assumptions (C_i) will have the general form

$$C_i(x): p_1(x) = 0 \,\&\, p_2(x) = 0 \,\&\, ... \,\&\, p_n(x) = 0.$$

An idealizational law L_i is derived from a real situation when we have a complete list of factual conditions (C_f) together with an idealizational equation of the form $p_n(x) = 0$ to account for each factor. Adapting Krajewski (1977), it can be represented as follows:

$$L_i: \forall x[C_f(x) \,\&\, p_1(x) = 0 \,\&\, p_2(x) = 0 \,\&\, ... \,\&\, p_n = 0 \to F(x) = 0].[8]$$

In order to test the idealizational law that we have established, we need to transform it by adding back the factors $(p_1 - p_n)$ which we have removed; which is to 'concretize' it. This process alters our idealized law of functional dependence $F(x) = 0$ making it more complex as more factors are added to it as the law is made increasingly concrete. Concretizing assumptions have the general form $p_i(x) \geq 0$.

A series of concretizations will have this general pattern:

$$L_i: \forall x[C_f(x) \,\&\, p_1(x) = 0 \,\&\, p_2(x) = 0 \,\&\, ... \,\&\, p_n = 0 \to F(x) = 0]$$
$$L^{(1)}_i: \forall x[C_f(x) \,\&\, p_1(x) \geq 0 \,\&\, p_2(x) = 0 \,\&\, ... \,\&\, p_n = 0 \to F^{(1)}(x) = 0]$$
$$L^{(2)}_i: \forall x[C_f(x) \,\&\, p_1(x) \geq 0 \,\&\, p_2(x) \geq 0 \,\&\, ... \,\&\, p_n = 0 \to F^{(2)}(x) = 0]$$
$$...$$
$$L_f: \forall x[C_f(x) \,\&\, p_1(x) \geq 0 \,\&\, p_2(x) \geq 0 \,\&\, ... \,\&\, p_n \geq 0 \to F^{(n)}(x) = 0]$$

The final stage in the series gives us L_f, which is the complete concretization of L_i. In theory, it describes the conditions necessary for a completely accurate empirical test of the idealizational law L_i.[9]

5.4 Objections to idealizational methodologies

A difficulty for the idealization approach to the methodology of science is that the practice of scientists simply does not reflect the rigour that idealizational accounts of scientific methodology suggest. Actual scientific practice diverges from idealizational models in at least three ways. First, scientists do not construct complete lists of possible interfering causal factors to account for when investigating real phenomena. Not only do they not do this now, it seems most unlikely that they would ever do so. How could we ever have grounds to be certain that we had considered all possible causal factors that might go into determining an effect? Second, sometimes even when scientists are aware of minor discrepancies between their favoured ideal explanatory models and empirical evidence, they do not bother to account for such discrepancies in their calculations. Instead they argue that the effect of some interfering causes is not significant enough to trouble with, or that, even though they cannot explain some results in detail, the explanatory model they are utilising is the only plausible one and that, no doubt, anomalies are caused by interference of so-far-unidentified factors which they do not regard as significant. Third, scientists frequently do not make exact calculations as to the magnitude of the effect of postulated interfering causes. Rather, they are often satisfied with rough and ready measures. A further defect of idealizational methodology is that it assumes that interfering causes can simply be subtracted to determine a remainder. However, it is not clear that causes always interact in a cumulative, vector-additive way.

Despite the preceding objections, I agree with Cartwright that Nowak's method of idealization is right in outline. It is something of a mistake to think of the method of idealization as directly describing science as it is. We should think of the method of idealization not as a method guiding the practice of scientists at a given point in time, but as an ideal of method constitutive of good scientific practice. When it comes to a comparison of competing scientific explanations, one important consideration will be comparison of the methods used to arrive at each of the rival explanations. All things being equal, we will prefer one explanation over another if we have reason to believe that the first was arrived at by methods of investigation more closely conforming to our constitutive ideal of method than the second explanation.

I hold that the virtues which we intuitively ascribe to scientific method are the same ones as those that are constituted by the ideal of practice needed to achieve precise idealization. Consider a comparison of two rival explanations of the same phenomenon. Was the first explanation arrived at by a process in which more possible causal factors were considered than the other explanation? Was the first explanation arrived at by a process in which the attempt was made to quantify more of the effects of known interfering causes than the rival explanation? Did the process by which the first explanation was arrived at include more exact calculations of the effects of interfering causes than the second explanation? Was the first explanation arrived at by a procedure which tested for more possible unexpected complications arising from the interaction of different causal factors than was the case in the second explanation? If the balance of other considerations is that the two explanations are judged to be equally appealing, then, when the answers to the above questions are all affirmative, it is clear that the first explanation is to be preferred to the second. The first has been arrived at by a method which more closely approximates to what it is to be a methodologically superior scientific explanation, according to the idealizational model of scientific practice.

Here is another way in which intuitions can be tweaked in favour of my constitutivity of method defence of the idealizational approach. Take any explanation in science and ask yourself this question: Would you have reason to be more certain of the correctness of that explanation if it was supplemented in the four ways described? I think it is intuitively obvious that any scientific explanation is more likely to be true if we: (1) consider and reject more possible alternate causal constituents that it excludes, than have been so far considered; (2) calculate more exactly the effects of interfering factors rather than resorting to approximation; (3) exactly calculate the influence of more of the factors that we know to be interfering with our results, rather than be satisfied with the belief that they are insignificant; and (4) determine more exactly how causes interfere with one another, rather than simply adding up their presumed contribution to the magnitude of an effect.

Despite the above argument there may remain one source of misgiving about the constitutive-ideal account of idealization. This is that we can never be certain that we have drawn up complete lists of possible causal factors for a given effect, so we will never be able to draw up complete lists of ways in which all possible causal factors interact. The ideal that I say is guiding scientific practice is one that can never be attained.

I maintain that our inability to attain the goal of perfect scientific method is no reason to suppose that there is not such a goal guiding us. Analogous problems recur in a variety of situations in which behaviour is goal-oriented. For example, historians and archaeologists aim to collect as much empirical evidence as possible about their chosen time and place of study, despite knowing in advance that they will never be certain that they can ever have a complete assemblage of all artefacts remaining from an era, nor, if they did, that it would provide them with sufficient evidence to form a complete list of all events that occurred within that era, nor that they could ever be certain that such a list was complete. The historian, no less than the scientist, is guided by a goal that she knows in advance will never be attained, only approached. But this is no reason to doubt that history is improved as its practitioners approach this ideal of a complete empirical base for history, and hence no reason to doubt that the ideal of a complete empirical base for history is a constitutive ideal for the practice of historians.

I have interpreted the method of idealization as embodying a constitutive ideal guiding research. The method is distanced from actual scientific practice in a number of other ways as well. Nowak considers several methodological assumptions, each of which needs to be justified if the methodology is to be thoroughly defended (1980, Part III). Importantly, it presumes that secondary factors can be fully listed and properly individuated. It also presumes that the only goal of researchers is to explain facts acquired by observation, and it presumes that researchers can make observations which are not importantly distorted by any theoretical presuppositions which they may have. As Nowak makes clear, the method of idealization is itself idealizational (Nowak 1980, p. 111).

5.5 Experimentation and idealization

Cartwright (1992) holds that under certain conditions, principally in laboratories, causal capacities can be 'laid bare' for us to see. In this complex disorderly world the places at which we can observe causal capacities in action are few and far between. In the laboratory, scientists are able to rearrange nature so as to bring capacities to the 'surface of reality'. However, Cartwright does not commit herself to the view that precise experimentation is necessary for the determination of the existence of capacities. She could not consistently be committed to such a view, as she endorses the capacity claims of econometrists in *Nature's Capacities...*, and econometrists do not perform precise laboratory-style experiments.

Unlike Cartwright, who enables us to account for the importance of experimentation in science, Nowak's position carries the implausible implication that experimentation is effectively redundant. Nowak follows Marx in holding that rigorous idealizational thinking is a substitute for experimentation. In Marx's words:

> [in] the analysis of economic forms ... neither microscopes nor chemical reagents are of use. The force of abstraction must replace both (Marx 1968a, p. 8).

Nowak and Marx's faith in the ability of the human mind to idealize correctly by careful thinking carries the implication that experimentation is redundant. Why spend vast amounts of money to allow scientists to build and operate specialised equipment if 'the forces of abstraction' can do the same thing for the lesser cost of mental labour? This faith leads to the bad consequence that it stops us from being able to distinguish between appropriately applied idealizational thinking and misapplied idealizational thinking. Furthermore it renders attempted dismissals of false idealizational thinking highly problematic. Nowak (1980, p. 10) follows Marx in explaining the shortcomings of Ricardo's economic theory by arguing that Ricardo does not pursue idealizational thinking far enough; a criticism which seems to carry the absurdly optimistic implication that any rigorous application of idealizational reasoning will lead to correct idealization. While Nowak holds that the method of idealization reveals the truth of Marx's law of value, mainstream economists categorically reject this law and would probably want to say that a methodology which ends up endorsing it must be an implausible one.

In regard to the importance of experimentation to the idealizational exportation of capacity claims, I argue against both Nowak and Cartwright (if her claim that capacities are 'laid bare' is to be taken literally). Against Nowak, I hold that the correct application of the method of idealization will not itself guarantee correct results. Against Cartwright, I hold that experimental science typically does not make capacities observable. Even in the clearest examples of experimental demonstration of causal relations, there is still a need to interpret the data presented. Experiments bring causal capacities closer to the empirical surface of reality, but typically they do not 'lay them bare' for us to see; although an ideal experiment would do that. Rather, experiments make the interpretive work of the mind considerably easier, by shortening the conceptual distance between idealized causal factors and actual data.

Consider a very simple example of a laboratory experiment, the high school vacuum tube demonstration. A clear glass vacuum tube is produced with a feather inside it, as well as a denser object. The tube is turned upright, and contrary to our expectations both objects accelerate downwards at equivalent rates, apparently hitting the bottom of the tube at the same time.

Normally feathers and dense objects fall towards the earth at different rates and in different patterns. In the vacuum tube the air is removed, and along with it its capacity to interfere with the feather's fall. An interfering factor is identified and it is removed, apparently demonstrating to the naked eye that there exists an underlying regularity; different objects are attracted towards the Earth at the very same rate. This result is unexpected on a first viewing, and hence impressive. It is so impressive that we risk overlooking some of the interpretive aspects of our observed outcome, at the same time as we grasp the importance of the experiment. The first of these is that our vacuum tube does not contain a true vacuum. By our own theoretical standards it cannot be a true vacuum as we do not believe that these exist. Rather, we believe that it is a near vacuum. For the purposes of providing a dramatic visual demonstration, it works well enough, but it is only an approximation to a vacuum. Presumably, within the near vacuum, the feather's fall remains more affected by whatever air resistance remains than does that of the heavier object, and so it still takes slightly longer to fall than the heavier object does. However, this difference is no longer visible to the naked eye, so the two objects appear to fall at the same rate. Nevertheless, we have not fully accounted for the entirety of the difference between the rate at which feathers actually fall and the rate at which we would expect them to fall given our idealizational hypothesis.

The problem just discussed leads to a second problem which can easily be overlooked in the explanation of the vacuum tube demonstration. The experiment is usually presented as a raw comparison of the magnitude of two rates, the acceleration of the feather and that of the denser object. Strictly, however, there are three rates to be taken into consideration: the rate of fall of the feather, that of the denser object, and that of ideal objects which are not subject to air resistance at all. Real dense objects in near vacuums are subject to air resistance, but their motion typically approximates to that of ideal objects that are free of air resistance. In order for idealizational arguments to succeed unproblematically we must be able to compare a real result with one that is by our own admission ideal. A direct comparison of this sort is not available to us. In actual practice we must settle for the comparison of the real with other real results. The capacity of objects to fall towards the surface of the earth at a consistent rate has not literally been presented to our eyes; instead we have achieved a good approximation from which we infer to the behaviour of the ideal object.

The vacuum tube case was a very clean case of idealization in comparison to most instances of experimentation, particularly the complex 'cutting edge' cases in physics which Cartwright discusses. In the vacuum tube experiment we had to remove just one interfering factor from consideration to apparently reveal an underlying capacity. The dramatic quality of this demonstration is very impressive, but the visual spectacle is not itself what makes the demonstration convincing. Also important are the plausibility and the theoretical independence of the experiment's auxiliary assumptions; that air resistance really is substantially diminished in the vacuum tube, and that there is no other factor significantly interfering with the manifestation of the force of gravity on the feather.

The vacuum tube example shows us an instance of a neat experimental solution to the problem of calculating the magnitude of an interfering factor. Often the scientist is not able to find an experimental solution to this problem and must simply make assumptions about the magnitude of interfering factors. Consider, for example, Eratosthenes' famous calculation of the diameter of the Earth. Eratosthenes made a calculation of the diameter of the Earth on the basis of three pieces of information: the distance between Alexandria and Syene, the fact that the direct journey from Alexandria to Syene was aligned north-south, and the difference in angle of direct sunlight falling on the two places at a given time. The difference in angle of light observed at the two different places enabled him to calculate the proportion of a circle's arc carved out over the distance between them. Knowing that distance, he was then able to calculate the circumference of the Earth and so determine its diameter, when he made two explicit auxiliary assumptions: That the Sun is infinitely far away from the Earth (and so rays of light striking the Earth's surface at different places are parallel to one another); and that the Earth is a perfect sphere.

Eratosthenes did not believe that the Sun was infinitely distant from the Earth; rather he believed that the Sun was far enough from the Earth that any two rays of light striking the earth's surface were approximately parallel. He did not know how far away the Sun was from the Earth, and for the purposes of his calculation he did not need to. What he needed to know was that it was far enough away that he could ignore the divergence of its rays from parallel, and this he had independent reason to believe. In this example an interfering factor has not been exactly quantified; rather it has been calculated to be within a non-significant range, and then idealized away to simplify subsequent calculations.

In successful experiments we are able to identify a causal capacity that we have reasons to believe to be near the 'empirical surface' of reality. But even in the case of the simplest and clearest experiments, the mind needs to perform substantial work to infer abductively to the existence of capacities. Experiments greatly extend the range and accuracy of idealizational techniques, and thereby enhance considerably the ability of science to export causal capacity claims. But they do not do this by literally exposing causal capacities for us to see.

5.6 Idealization and scientific progress

To be able to provide powerful explanatory and predictive fundamental laws, scientific reasoning needs to become idealizational. To become the practitioners of a higher-order discipline, the scientists within a discipline need to master techniques for isolating causal factors in controlled environments and exporting that information to uncontrolled worldly situations. These are the techniques of idealization. Currently, only the laboratory sciences have been transformed into such higher-order sciences. In the laboratory, scientists have learned how to manipulate entities and intervene in their activities in such a way as to enable rigorous idealizational reasoning. The transformation of a scientific discipline so as to enable the use of idealizational techniques constitutes a form of progress in science.

A view which I do not want to endorse is the view that adherence to the process of scientific idealization guarantees that we will arrive at absolute truth; that idealizations of causal factors 'carve reality' at just the joints that it happens to have, and not at other places. Quite apart from my general rejection of fundamentalism, this seems too optimistic and too restrictive a requirement for a scientific methodology. Newtonian physics looks like an example of the outcome of a systematic set of idealizations that is at least as rigorous as other examples of successful science; indeed, for many years it was upheld as the paradigm of rigorous scientific practice. Yet we now believe, in light of developments in relativistic physics, that Newtonian physics is only as accurate as it is because the results it gives us are very good approximations to a range of outcomes that happened to be the ones that Newton and those who developed his approach were confronted with; those which occur when relativistic space-time approximates to Euclidean space and absolute time.

The relation between Boyle's law and van der Waal's law is an example of a relation between two laws that can be explained idealizationally. Boyle's law is, in effect, van der Waal's law applied to gases that are idealized in that they lack intermolecular forces; and Boyle's law can be concretized into van der Waal's law.[10] The same cannot be said for the relationship between Newtonian and relativistic physics. Knowledge of relativistic physics allows us to explain why Newtonian physics should approximate to the outcomes that we now expect for a given range, but not because Newtonian physics is an idealization of relativistic physics. It is not a theory that is idealizationally related to relativistic physics, in that it is not a relativistic physics stripped of one or more parameters. Rather, relativistic physics is a refigured physics which Newtonian physics approximates to, in some cases, but which Newtonian physics could not be concretized into.

Galileo wrote as if clear careful idealization leads straightforwardly to truth, and Nowak appears to write with the same assumption in mind. In any case we should interpret Nowak as being committed to the belief that the method of idealization provides us with direct access to the absolute truth. After all, the aim of his work is to show that Marx's theory of political economy is an idealizational theory, and that it is also a true description of the forces driving history. However, we must be careful in judging Nowak. Nowak (1980) holds a Hegelian view of truth, on which a non-true theory, from which results are derived that approximate to the absolute truth, can be said to be true if it constitutes a stage in the development of a lineage of theories which come successively closer to the absolute truth. On a Hegelian account of truth, from the standpoint of relativistic physics, Newtonian mechanics can be said to be (approximately) true in that it provides us with a set of results that approximate to a range of results that a theory which is truer would also predict and in that it is part of the genealogy of that truer theory.

When Nowak's Hegelian view of truth is used to inform a view of the progress of science, he ends up endorsing a view of progress in science which is sensitive to Kuhn's historical insights. Ascension to absolute truth is clearly not guaranteed on this reinterpretation of Kuhn, which Nowak summarises as follows:

(a) An idealizational theory that already can explain many phenomena is constructed in spite of the fact that at the same time there are many phenomena contradicting it. The latter contradict the approximations of the starting laws of the theory.

(b) The theory in question is concretized. As a result an explanation of many phenomena from the ones that contradict the approximation of the starting laws is obtained. The latter turn out to contradict the theory only *prima facie*.

(c) This results in spreading among the adherents of the paradigm an opinion that all the phenomena that contradict the theory will turn out to be only *prima facie* contradicting it.

(d) Only when more and more phenomena contradicting any concretization of the theory in question are discovered, and the formerly well-known ones that contradict it cannot be explained in its subsequent concretizations, a crisis takes place. Scientists gradually stop believing that further concretizations of the paradigm will prove that the incompatibilities with experience are only apparent.

(e) The crisis brings about the formulation of a new theory that explains the phenomena that actually contradicted the former one. The new theory also becomes a paradigm, etc. (Nowak 1980, p. 90).

Nowak's method of confirmation by concretization was developed with an awareness of the difficulty of confirmation in the face of possible multiple interfering factors in a given situation. When we accept the difficulty of approaching the ideal of rigour of the idealizational method in examples of what we nowadays think of as good science, we see that there is room for the tolerance of anomalies for long periods of time, on pragmatic grounds.

Suppose a particular concretization apparently refutes a theory. If it is a typical concretization, it is an approximate calculation, deficient in any or all of the ways discussed earlier in this chapter. Given that we have no better theory available, it will be rational to hold on to our theory rather than abandon it. This pragmatic limitation on the possibility of idealization makes Nowak's conception of scientific progress look similar to Imré Lakatos's (1970) conception of scientific progress, developed explicitly as a way of responding to Kuhn (1962). On Nowak's Lakatosian view a theory can be retained despite known anomalies (*prima facie* contradictions). As long as progress is being made in the process of addressing anomalies, we continue to accept the theory. It is only when some of the anomalies prove intractable that we begin to doubt that they are only apparent anomalies. At that stage we begin to search for a new theory with the hope that it will be one with which we can achieve more progress in explaining the given empirical evidence.

Broadly, I concur with Nowak's Lakatosian view of progress in science. However, there are two ways in which my view of scientific progress differs from his. First, I think that Nowak's account only applies to the laboratory sciences. The social sciences and the life sciences are pre-idealizational. Nowak is motivated by his aim of depicting Marx's socio-economic theory as scientific, on a par with other idealizational sciences. While it is possible for non-laboratory sciences to utilise idealizational techniques (which Marx does), in order to be reliable the method of idealization requires that we begin with precise measurement of the magnitude of causal factors. At present the non-laboratory sciences cannot provide the requisite level of precision for effective exportation of invariant causal capacity claims. Marx's economic theory is idealizational in that it critically depends upon an attempt to determine the magnitude of the contribution of interfering causal factors in order to uncover the laws governing abstract economic behaviour. However, the inexactness of the idealizational calculations made in abstracting the primary factors of economic behaviour renders attempts to concretize them unconfirmable. Unsurprisingly, Marxist economics lacks genuine predictive value.

The second way in which my account of progress in science differs from Nowak's is that I reject Nowak's Leninist essentialism. Nowak appears confident that his methodology, despite being as liberal as Lakatos's, is one that can be relied upon to discover the true essences of things. I think that it is readily apparent that an account of progress that is permissive enough to accommodate Kuhnian paradigm shifts cannot be one that we can rely upon to ground confidence that scientific method will guarantee our ascent to absolute truths. Nowak's essentialism is a hang over from his Marxist heritage. His insistence that the method of idealization is applicable in the non-experimental sciences is a product of his desire to justify Marxism as scientific. In the process of attempting to justify Marxism as scientific, Nowak has described a philosophy of science which captures the relationship between experimental situations and worldly situations. This is an important advance in the sophistication of the philosophy of science, and in epistemology in general. However, Nowak's Marxist heritage has led him to draw unsustainable conclusions from his otherwise valuable work.

We are now in a position to summarise the methodological position outlined in this chapter, along with the previous one. Scientific reasoning, like common-sense reasoning about the external world, centrally involves the attribution of causal capacities to objects, and the subsequent exportation of those capacity claims to other objects. Attributed capacities need to be relatively stable and enduring: they need to be invariant, in Woodward's terminology. Common-sense reasoning, along with causal attribution in the life sciences and the social sciences, only enables rough and ready exportation. In order for capacity claims to be exportable into complex worldly situations in such a way as to enable the determination of the exact magnitudes of the contribution of many different causal factors, a science needs to be transformed; it needs to become idealizational. The laboratory sciences are idealizational sciences. They enable the precise measurement of the magnitude of particular causal factors. This, in turn, enables the development of powerful predictive explanations in these sciences and its absence explains why powerful predictive explanations are lacking in other sciences. Sciences progress by becoming idealizational. However, the transformation of a pre-idealizational science into an idealizational science is not all there is to say about progress in science. Nor is the employment of an accurate idealizational methodology a guarantor of explanatory success. Within idealizational sciences there is progress, but it is not progress that guarantees the ascent to truth. Instead it is progress along broadly Lakatosian pragmatic lines.

Notes

---

1   We should not overstate the predictive successes of scientific explanations in complex situations, for reasons outlined in Chapter Two.
2   Koyré (1943) argues that Galileo saw himself as advancing metaphysical Platonist conclusions against the Aristotelians of his era.
3   This project is pursued today by Bas van Fraassen, who targets 'the dying metaphor of law' as a refuge of 'inner necessities' (van Fraassen 1989, p. 6).
4   See Dijksterhuis (1986). Also Koyré (1943) and Kuhn (1977).
5   It is worth noting, however, in support of Nowak's interpretation of Marx, that Marx saw himself as methodologically distinct from 'vulgar empiricist', or 'bourgeois philosophers', as the following quote, contrasting two distinct methods of investigation, reveals:

> One of these conceptions fathoms the inner connection, the physiology, so to speak, of the bourgeois system, whereas the other takes the external phenomena of life, as they seem and appear and merely describes, catalogues, recounts and arranges them under formal definitions (Marx, 1968b, part II, p. 165).

6   Nowak (1989) considers abstraction and idealization as particular types of the broader category of 'deformational procedures'.
7   Nowak (1992) appears to favour Krajewski's (1977) formalisation over his own of Nowak (1980).
8   Krajewski (1977) only considers laws of synchronic quantitative dependence between a set of parameters (a, b, ...) of ideal objects (x) of the general form $F[a(x), b(x), ...] = 0$, which he abbreviates as $F(x) = 0$.
9   Krajewski uses the schema described to concretize Boyle's Law into van der Waal's Law. See Krajewski (1977, p. 24).
10   See Krajewski (1977, pp. 24-5 and pp. 38-40).

6 The End of the World as We Know It

6.1 The unity of science

I have argued for the possibility of progress in science without the presumption that there is some underlying orderliness in the world, be it the orderliness implicit in modern conceptions of laws of nature, or any other metaphysical presumption about the structuredness of the constituents of the universe. On my view, we can acquire reliable useful information about the world, without making the presumption that the world has a basic level of organisation. We come to know about aspects of the world piecemeal, and we need no presumption that those pieces will fit together in any particular way.

Twentieth century empiricists have typically related progress to the unification of the sciences. I will briefly examine a variety of different ways to conceive of the unification of the sciences and show how those approaches differ from the one which I take. It will emerge that I am not explicitly hostile to the possibility of unification of science. I will show that a metaphysics of disunity does not preclude us from holding the unification of the sciences to be a desirable goal.

The terms 'unity of science' and 'unification of science' are sometimes used to refer to any feature that the sciences might happen to have in common. For example, it is widely held that there is a methodological unity of science. Sometimes it is felt that there is a pressing need to find an identifying feature definitive of science, in order to effect a demarcation between science and non-science. There is also another sense of the term 'unity of science' which we will be concerned with here. Broadly, the term 'unity of science', in the sense that will concern us, refers to the hypothesis that the different sciences could or perhaps will one day become synthesised into one greater science. The hope expressed by those who advocate unification of the sciences is hope for the merging of the different sciences into a single comprehensive body of theory. In such a unified science, each branch of science would gain credibility from being securely attached to all other divisions of science. An influential blueprint for the unification of science is the logical empiricist reductionist programme expressed in Putnam and Oppenheim's (1958) *Unity of Science as a Working Hypothesis*.

In the 1960s and 1970s the hegemony of Logical Empiricism in Anglo-American philosophy was under attack from many fronts, and the unity of the sciences thesis was one such front. A well-known attack on this thesis was Jerry Fodor's article *Special Sciences, or the Disunity of Science as a Working Hypothesis* (1974). Fodor equates the unity of science thesis with the view that '... all true theories in the special sciences should reduce to physical theories in the "long run"' (Fodor 1974, p. 77). This formulation looks flexible enough to capture the two complementary means by which the complete unification of science into physical science could be achieved: reduction and elimination. If a theory in one of the special sciences is true, then, according to an advocate of the unity of science thesis, as conceived of by Fodor, that theory will be reducible to physics.[1] If it is not true, then it will eventually be eliminated from complete science.

Typically, advocates of unity of science theses have taken the view that reduction to physics of many or all of the various special sciences is attainable, and elimination is usually appealed to only after the reduction of some particular theory in a special science has been shown to fail. Much of the cut and thrust of argument about the potential unification of the sciences has focused on the possibility of reduction. The reduction of one body of scientific knowledge to another would not present important philosophical problems if the two bodies of knowledge are homogeneous. In such cases successful reduction is merely a case of logical derivation. On occasions this is effectively what happens in science: for example, Galileo's laws of the motion of free-falling terrestrial bodies were successfully absorbed into Newtonian mechanics and gravitational theory. The terms employed in Galileo's laws were all replaceable by convenient close approximates in Newtonian theory. More commonly, however, a scientific treatment of some subject matter which we would like to reduce to a primary science turns out to contain terms which are not directly derivable from the terms of the primary science. In such cases we must argue for the plausibility of translation of the terms of the higher-order science into the terms of the lower-order science. Consider, for example, the reducibility of the common-sense use of the term *temperature* into the terminology of kinetic theory. If a lay person is informed that the temperature of an object simply is the mean kinetic energy of the molecules that the object is composed of, she may well protest. She may say that, although the motion of its constituent molecules may explain why the object is hot or cold, the temperature of the object is something that she experiences; something quite different from molecular motion. To convince her that temperature really is nothing more than mean kinetic energy we would need to argue for the translation of heteronomous terms.[2]

Reductionist logical empiricists did not generally argue for the direct reduction of all of the special sciences to physics. Rather, they argued for the eventual reduction of all sciences to physics via a series of microreductions of one science into another. According to Putnam and Oppenheim (1958, p. 9), there are at least six levels of organisation of the world: social groups, living things, cells, molecules, atoms, and elementary particles, each level corresponding to a different grouping of sciences. Putnam and Oppenheim allow that there may be other levels of organisation, but they maintain that there is a finite number of levels, that there is a unique lowest level into which all microreductions will eventually reduce, and that every element of a level reduces to the next lowest level. Complete reduction would be achieved when every element at all levels of organisation has been reduced to a level which has itself been completely reduced to the unique lowest level.

These considerations sound as though they are derived from an explicitly metaphysical view of the world. As such it would seem that Putnam and Oppenheim (1958) were placing themselves in open conflict with the staunchly anti-metaphysical progenitors of the positivist unity of the sciences movement, such as Carnap and Neurath. In fact, Putnam and Oppenheim evade such a conflict. They describe the levels of organisation they propose as *universes of discourse*: semantic constructs rather than real entities (Putnam and Oppenheim 1958, p. 9). Nevertheless, they make very little effort to avoid the appearance of realism about their proposed levels of organisation of the world. The effect on subsequent discussion of reductionism was to encourage more explicitly metaphysical formulations of the mechanisms by which unification of the sciences could be carried out, and to focus attention on a strategy to make progress towards unification of science: the strategy of microreduction.

A microreduction is a relationship between theories. It is the mapping of one theory onto a theory at the next lowest level of organisation. The exact means by which Logical Empiricists would accomplish microreductions was an open topic, but the central characteristic of all proposed micro-reductions is that one or more of the structural features of a higher-order theory would be shown to be isomorphic with special cases of a lower-order theory. The most influential reductionist programme of micro-reduction was nomic reductionism, in which the laws of a higher-order theory were to be shown to be isomorphic with the laws of a lower-order theory by means of the identification of bridging laws which would translate the laws of the higher-order body of knowledge into the laws of the more basic one. For example, a theory T1 might contain the predicate F among its terms, while a higher-order theory T2 contains a predicate G referring to the same subject matter. An appropriate bridging law would tell us that whenever an object has property F it also has property G. Then the bridging law could be used to translate statements in T1 which contained predicate F into statements in T2 which contained predicate G. The possibility of this project succeeding was based on the assumption that a significant number of pairs of scientific theories were isomorphic in structure, an assumption which examination of likely candidate theories for reduction showed to be quite naive. As a result, debate about the possibility of microreduction became increasingly complex, as participants haggled over what exactly would constitute evidence of the reducibility of one science into another.[3]

6.2 An aim for science

As I have described it, the unity of the sciences project might seem to have been directed at predicting the future of science. As such, it looks like the sort of project that philosophers ought not to be engaged in. Surely philosophers don't know in advance that the sciences are going to be unified. Whether the sciences will become unified or not is, in significant part, an empirical question and philosophers are typically not well posit-ioned to answer empirical questions, especially empirical questions about the distant future. However, when we look at the work of prominent advocates of a unity of the sciences thesis — Neurath, Carnap, and Putnam — they all freely admit that we cannot know in advance that the sciences will become unified. They all appeal to unity as an appropriate *aim* for the development of science. So, unity of the sciences is a prescriptive rather than a merely descriptive enterprise. Advocates of unity of the science theses do, of course, want to convince us that unity of the sciences is a significant descriptive possibility for science; however, the philosophically important question lurking behind the unity of the sciences project is the question of why the aim of unifying the sciences is a desirable goal at all.

An initially plausible fundamentalist reason to think that we should aim to unify the sciences is that there is only one world which science aims to represent, and that world is the physical world. If science is ever to give us a completely satisfactory representation of this one world, then science will have to be unified. If we are physicalists, then, it would seem that we must be committed to finding a unified science. Against this line of reasoning, Fodor (1974) argues that the acceptance of physicalism does not entail the reduction of all the special sciences to physics, and hence acceptance of physicalism does not require acceptance of the goal of unity of the sciences. Fodor (1974) argues that when a physicalist accepts token physicalism, rather than type physicalism, she can avoid commitment to reductionism. Token physicalism is the view that the types of higher-order sciences supervene on an open-ended disjunction of tokens of the lower-order science. So, for example, a psychological type such as pain does not supervene on any one particular brain state but on an open-ended disjunction of possible different realiser brain states.

Fodor (1974) asks us to construe the relationship between higher-order and lower-order sciences as one which we would nowadays refer to as a relationship of supervenience rather than reducibility. Supervenience is, almost exclusively, a philosophers' concept which was popularised by Davidson and others in the 1970s. Since then there has been a proliferation of different formulations of the supervenience relation. Kim (1991) identifies three components that are common to the majority of these formulations. There are:

Covariance: Supervenient properties covary with their subvenient, or base, properties. In particular, indiscernibility in respect of the base properties entails indiscernibility in respect of the supervenient properties.

Dependency: Supervenient properties are dependent on, or are determined by, their base properties.

Nonreducibility: Supervenience is to be consistent with the irreducibility of the supervenient properties to their base properties. (Kim 1991, p. 9).

If we accept token physicalism, then it seems we can accept that the laws of a higher-order science are true, and we can accept that the laws of physics are true; and we can accept that the laws of the higher-order science are not reducible to the laws of physics. And we can do all of this without entailing

the existence of any mysterious emergent properties which would jeopard-
ise physicalism.

Still, unificationist intuitions will not be completely dispelled by Fodor's
argument against reductionism. The unificationist will insist that even if the
relationship between higher-order types and physical tokens is infinitely
disjunctive in logical space, in the actual world there will be a finite number
of these disjuncts that could realise a supervening type. So, returning to our
example, even through it is true that there is a potentially unlimited
number of realiser brain states for pain, there will actually be practical
limits to their diversity. There will be only so many ways in which a human
brain can be so arranged as to realise pain, and even if we allow that
silicon-based Martians can experience pain, there will be only so many
ways in which their silicon brains can be arranged. There will be a limit to
the elements in the disjunct characterising the physical realiser tokens for
the type pain, and, given that limit, we will be potentially able to give a
complete redescription of pain in the language of microphysics.[4]

Now, as we don't know what actually exists in the entirety of the
physical realm, the only way the foregoing attempt to block infinite
disjunctiveness could succeed was if it was grounded in an appeal to some
sort of constraints on physical possibility. But what constraints *are* there,
implicit in the concept of physical possibility, which could be used to
restrict the ways in which a higher-order type may be realised? In my view,
the intuition that there are inherent limitations on physical possibility
derives from the deeper fundamentalist intuition that there exists just one
coherent, limited, level of reality. The conviction that acceptance of
physicalism has as a consequence the acceptance of the unity of the sciences
thesis implicitly assumes that physicalism commits one to a strong
presumption of orderliness. On this view, it is because the physical world is
tightly ordered at one level that higher levels of organisation are presumed
to be reducible to that lower order. They are merely complex recom-
binations of the initial orderliness of the lower level.[5]

Can we seriously cast aside the presumption that the world is orderly at
a basic level? As we saw in Chapter Two a number of philosophers have
done so, Cartwright and Dupré being the most prominent contemporary
advocates of disunity. Dupré (1993) asks us, as Fodor does, to accept the
disunity of the sciences. However, unlike Fodor, Dupré explicitly advocates
the acceptance of a disunified ontology. But how could a disordered ontology even produce what order there is in our world? Nancy Cartwright's
metaphor of a patchwork world, discussed in Chapter Two, is helpful here.
Our world might be a world in which there exists a disunified patchwork of

laws of nature, with what laws there are being the expression of relatively stable and invariant capacities where these happen to be found. If we had created the world, then this is probably not how we would have chosen to make it. But if we believe that the world is out there waiting to be discovered, then we are not entitled to dismiss the possibility that we live in a world governed by a disunified patchwork of sometimes highly localised laws.

6.3 Orderliness and the metaphysics of disunity

The presumption that the world is orderly leads to a motivation for a unified science. But, interestingly, the acceptance of the possibility of metaphysical disorder can also lead to a motivation to find a unified science. As we saw in Chapter One, the possibility of metaphysical disorder, often conflated with scepticism, has generally been perceived to be dangerous, and the demonstration of the unity of science is invoked as a response to the threat posed by disorder. Broadly, there are two strategies for attempting to defuse the threat raised by the possibility of metaphysical disorder that philosophers have pursued: the Hegelian and the Kantian. The main difference between the two is that the Kantian attempts to show how the threat of disorder can be defused now, while the Hegelian attempts to show that it can be defused over time.

Kant holds that the threat of disorder is avoided when humans impose order on the phenomenal world via the agency of reason. Reason carries out its work by imposing categories of thought on the world. To take the case of causality; we impose the quality of necessity on regularities between candidate causes and effects, and thereby construct causal relations. The Kantian presumption that knowledge is always schematic, even if it doesn't appear that way, has been influential in philosophy over the last two centuries. It received powerful opposition, from Hegel, and from a succession of nineteenth century idealist philosophers.

Hegel argues that Kant cannot be right about the power of reason to impose structure upon the phenomenal world, now. The different branches of human knowledge do not cohere with one another, and indeed are not internally coherent. Human knowledge, now, is riddled with contradictions. However, the different sciences will become unified, according to Hegel, in the process of history — the unfolding of the dialectic. Hegel historicises reason, but salvages Kant's impositional reason by relegating it to the end of history, when it becomes 'the Absolute'. Reason can be historicised if history is teleological and has as an end a state where the contradictions within knowledge are overcome and the different branches of human knowledge united.

Bradley preached an argument similar to Hegel's, the better part of a century after Hegel. Bradley held that knowledge, now, is laden with contradictions, but that these would be resolved in the unfolding of history, as we advance towards the realisation of the Absolute. For Bradley, the work of the dialectic is taken over by the doctrine of internal relations. Our thoughts about the world reveal coherence in the world, because the world is continuous with our thoughts about it.

For both Hegel and Bradley we have reason to be confident that we are on the road to the Absolute, because our collective thoughts constitute progress towards the Absolute. On their views, although we do not have a guarantee that we will ever reach the Absolute, we do seem to have a guarantee that we are progressing towards it, and progress towards the Absolute is sufficient to play the role of guarantor against the threat of disorder in the world, given that for idealists the world is indistinguishable from the sum of our collected thoughts. Unfortunately, however, neither Hegel's nor Bradley's version of idealism succeeds in guaranteeing progress towards the Absolute and thereby refuting the possibility of disorder. Hegel and Bradley do not make the Kantian move of presuming that we impose order on the world. Instead they make the subtler move of presuming order in aspects of the world which are supposed to play the role of guarantor of progress to the Absolute. Hegel makes unjustified presumptions about the orderliness of history in order to convince us that history is an agent of progress rather than merely an agent of change; and Bradley makes the same unjustified presumptions with regard to relations, for the same reasons.

It might be supposed that the positivist philosophers were Kantians about the unification of the sciences. Like Kant, Carnap, the leading figure in the Vienna Circle, saw himself as attempting to put a stop to metaphysical speculation, and saw the demonstration of the unity of knowledge as central to the rejection of metaphysics. Carnap's essay *Logical Foundations of the Unity of Science* (1955) outlines his anti-metaphysical version of reductionism. Reduction, on this view, is not ontological reduction to physics itself, but semantic reduction to physical language. The physical language is a convenience of science, and ultimately reduction to the language of 'observation-thing-predicates' is sought. This basic language should not be conflated with the language of pure phenomena that Carnap aimed to reduce science to in the *Aufbau*. Instead it is an expression of the conventional basis which we agree to be the most exacting level of description that we have achieved at a given time. The positivists looked for unity in the language of science, rather than in the world. As they were concerned to describe the 'logic of science', it might appear that they are in the business of explaining how we impose order on the world, as did Kant. But this appearance is illusory. If we were to impose order on the world via language, then we would need something like a coherent system of laws of scientific language to impose order with. However, in *Logical Foundations of the Unity of Science* (1955) Carnap stresses that there is no unity of laws at present. That must wait for the future. And although Carnap appeals to the unity of the language of science to show the possibility of the unity of the laws of science being achieved, he does not argue that the unity of the laws of science is guaranteed by the unity of the *language* of science. Instead he argues that the unity of the language of science is a necessary preliminary condition for the eventual unity of laws of science. I will go on to portray the positivist attitude towards the unity of the science as a position that vacillates between the Hegelian attitude towards the unity of the sciences and what I will refer to as a postmodern attitude of rejection of the goal of unification of the sciences.

6.4 *Positivism and postmodernism*

The development of the positivism of the Vienna Circle of the 1930s was manifested within the Circle as the struggle between two loose factions, which came to be known as the left and the right wing. The right wing, which defended the logical atomist conception of philosophy, was represented by Schlick. Neurath embodied the spirit of the left wing, emphasising the pragmatic and political character of science. Logical atomists, such as Schlick, had hoped to eliminate metaphysics from philosophy by traditional foundationalist means. Neurath emphasised the metaphysics implicit in Schlick and the early Wittgenstein's foundationalism, manifested in the presumption that statements in a language might latch on to atomic pieces of the world as if they were fortuitously appropriate for such a role. Against this image of philosophy, Neurath stressed the conventional character of language and especially the conventional character of its relation to empirical data. As debate continued, the left wing overcame the right. Neurath's key success was in shifting the stance of Rudolph Carnap.

That Neurath is a holist is well known, mainly due to the widespread usage of the metaphor of Neurath's boat. What is not well known is that, unlike holists of the mid-to-late twentieth century such as Quine and Davidson, Neurath did not presume the internal coherence of natural conceptual schemes. He explicitly fought against this presumption. Like postmodernist philosophers of recent times, Neurath emphasised the indeterminate character of terms within natural conceptual schemes. This point is borne out when we consider the metaphor of Neurath's boat in context:[6]

> We are like sailors who have to rebuild their ship on the open sea, without ever being able to dismantle it in dry-dock and reconstruct it from the best components. Only metaphysics can disappear without a trace. Imprecise 'verbal clusters' ['Ballungen'] are somehow always part of the ship. If imprecision is diminished at one place, it may well re-appear at another place to a stronger degree (Neurath 1932, p. 92).

It is not just any holism that sails in Neurath's boat. A holism which fails to acknowledge the indeterminate character of elements within our representational schemes is a holism stained with metaphysics and therefore, according to Neurath, as unacceptable to a thoroughgoing positivist as atomist foundationalism. Neurath's equation of metaphysics with the denial of indeterminacy within a conceptual scheme can also be seen in his attacks on a philosopher with whom he was to share a relationship of mutual animosity: Karl Popper. In a broadside against Popper's *Logik der Forschung* (1935), Neurath asserts that

> Popper blocks his own way to a full appreciation of the practice of research and the history of research to which his book is basically devoted. Namely, he does not use the *ambiguity* [Neurath's emphasis] of all factual sciences as the basis of his comments, but, following Laplace's spirit, as it were, aims at one unique distinguished system of statements as the pattern or paradigm of all the factual sciences (Neurath 1935, p. 121).[7]

Neurath's name is associated closely with the proposed development of an *Encyclopedia of Unified Science*. Neurath explicitly did not intend the encyclopedia to act as a proof that there was a single, absolute system of science to be found. Rather, he proposed a collection of currently diverse scientific works, which would assist scientists in building connections between the different sciences.[8]

In Neurath's words,

> [if] we reject the rationalistic anticipation of *the* system of the sciences, if we reject the notion of a philosophical system which is to legislate for the sciences,

what is the maximum co-ordination of the sciences which remains possible? The only answer that can be given for the time being is: An *Encyclopedia of the Sciences* (Neurath 1937, pp. 176-7).

The encyclopedia that Neurath laboured for was part of an ambitious political programme to put science to work to create a more just, more rational society. The role of scientists and philosophers in this project was to attempt to 'orchestrate' science (Neurath 1946). There were two chief means by which this orchestration was to be advanced. First, by regularly exchanging and updating ideas in the encyclopedia of science, and in the Unity of the Sciences conferences, of which there were several held before World War II. Second, by adopting artificial languages, which would operate to lessen the inherent dangers of ambiguity thrown up by indeterminacies of translation. The pragmatic Neurath rejected Carnap's idealistic call for the universal adoption of Esperanto, favouring the use of Logpu, a set of simplified versions of actual natural languages with a uniform logical structure.

The ambitions of the Vienna Circle's Unity of the Sciences project are closely related to Neurath's socialist politics. We should not, however, make the mistake of assuming that Neurath's encyclopedia project was separate from his general philosophy of science; as he makes clear in another attack on Popper, encyclopedism is central to his philosophical conception of science and of the indeterminacy of scientific language as it is now:

> If one wants to say that Popper starts from *model-systems*, one could say that we, on the other hand, start from *model-encyclopedias*; this would express from the outset that systems of clean statements are not put forward as the basis of our comments (Neurath 1935, p. 122).

Neurath's acknowledgement of the disunity of science now, coupled with his desire for unification, suggests a Hegelian outlook. But Neurath is not a Hegelian. For Hegelians, unification is constitutive of progress in the development of human understanding of the world. The unity of science plays no critical role in Neurath's philosophy, other than that of being a desirable goal independent of philosophical concerns. Neurath is not motivated by the threat of disorder to postulate an absolute, a definitive end of science; nor does he presume that we have any guarantee that we will achieve unity of the sciences in the long run.

Cat, Chang and Cartwright (1991) compare Neurath with recent post-empiricist (and, they say, postmodernist) philosophers, such as Sandra

Harding (1986) and John Dupré (1993). Harding and Dupré are suspicious of the motives of those who glorify science in general and the advocates of the unity of the sciences in particular, whom they see as agents of coercion, and whose politics are considered unacceptable in a pluralistic age. Dupré specifically rejects what he takes to be the metaphysical presumptions of the unity of the sciences movement. He takes his metaphysics of disunity to be incompatible with the goal of unification of the sciences. Dupré holds that 'no thesis of the unity of science can serve any legitimate purposes for which it might be intended' (Dupre 1993, p. 221) .

Cat, Chang and Cartwright (1991) observe that 'the picture of science which Neurath commended under the banner *unity* is very much the same as the one labelled *disunity* by its post-modern critics' (Cat, Chang and Cartwright 1991, p. 93). Their comparison of Dupré and Neurath is striking.[9] Both philosophers are physicalists, and pluralists, and both deny reductionism. Both Neurath and current postmodernist and post-empiricist philosophers acknowledge the disunity of science, now, but hold diametrically different attitudes towards the desirability of the goal of unification of science. These attitudes spring from different attitudes towards science as it is practised. Neurath placed his faith in science to help create a better world. Neurath was heavily involved in the politics of post-World-War-I Europe and, fired by the promise of socialism, he believed that unified science could help co-ordinate and focus political action. For Neurath, socialism was part of science, and

> socialism would gain if the political leaders could draw on socio-technical engineers who ... construct the economic organisation that would best realise the socialist economic plan (Neurath 1920, p. 226).[10]

Postmodernists are notoriously suspicious of authority, especially that of science. To them Neurath's faith in the power of science may seem hopelessly naive. It's not that postmodernists don't appreciate the power of science: they do, and they are very wary of it. What they do not share is Neurath's faith in our ability to harness the power of science.

Suspicion of science is nothing new, and Neurath did attempt to address it when the unity of the sciences project was attacked as imperialistic by Kallen, the inventor of Logpu. In Neurath's reply to Kallen he argues that a unified science with a unified language will have the effect of reducing the difference in power between scientific leaders and the general public (Neurath 1946, pp. 236-42). I doubt that he is right about that broad claim, but I think we must grant him at least this much: if the general public were able to comprehend science better there would be less scope for those holding power within science to abuse that power.

Neurath appeals to those who would be suspicious of science with the following words:

> The unity we have before us, as a goal for the encyclopedism of logical empiricism, is based on the actual store of expressions which people have in common all over the world. Its evolution would be based on conventions which could never be definite or authoritative as far as the aspirations of conscientious logical empiricists are concerned. Pluralism is the aura of this scientific world community of the common man. The encyclopedism of logical empiricism with the unified science encyclopedia are the children of the tolerant approach of democratic co-operation. It competes with no philosophy, and is anti-totalitarian through and through (Neurath 1946, p. 242).

When Neurath's optimism about our ability to harness science for our own ends is tempered by the acknowledgement that we need to be vigilant in the face of the temptation experienced by some or all of us to misuse the power that science gives us, we arrive at a position that I am happy to endorse.

What is inspiring about Neurath's philosophy is that it serves as an antidote to postmodern pessimism. I argued in Chapter One that post-modernists such as Rorty build their cases for abandoning modernist philosophy on a false totalising image of the history of philosophy. Neurath's pragmatic positivism shows how enlightenment ideals can be rationally pursued without making any of the metaphysical assumptions that fundamentalists actually make, and which non-fundamentalists such as Neurath are often wrongly accused of making by postmodernists.

In the spirit of Neurath, I deny that a proponent of the metaphysics of disunity should be hostile to the goal of unification of the sciences. What the proponent of the metaphysics of disunity should oppose is the fundamentalist's metaphysical prejudice in favour of the view that the world is unified. The proponent of the metaphysics of disunity should also oppose the presumption that we obtain knowledge of the world by a process that commits us to imposing unified structures of belief upon the diverse elements constituting the world. Knowledge is acquired piecemeal and does not require a framework in which to be fitted. However, the proponent of the metaphysics of disunity need not reject a preference for unification if that preference is motivated by concerns that are unrelated to fundamentalist ambitions.

Metaphysics and the Disunity of Scientific Knowledge

Are there philosophical reasons for us to prefer to find unity in the world, when we take seriously the idea that this might be a disunified world? I believe that there is at least one such reason, which follows directly from the idealizational account of causal attribution in science, outlined in Chapter Five. We are able to provide powerful explanations of worldly phenomena by exporting idealized capacity claims, made in the laboratory, into complex worldly situations. Such exportation is made considerably easier in parts of the world where we do discover underlying order. There, we can more accurately concretize ideal laws to account for the complexity of reality, and thereby better test those laws. When this occurs we do not have to make as many excuses for the divergence of reality from the predictions given by fundamental laws. For our explanatory purposes, we would prefer to find as much unity in the world as we can. But we can and should be ready to accept failure in our search for unity. This will be no disaster. For a long time scientists have shown us how to make do without the presumption that the world is unified. It is time for philosophers to follow their lead.

I began this book by arguing against the totalising history of philosophy of a postmodernist writer, Richard Rorty. I have ended it by presenting a pragmatist alternative to the anti-enlightenment stance of postmodernists, which I adapt from the philosophy of Otto Neurath. Neurath's Unification of the Sciences movement is driven by a faith in the power of science to emancipate and enlighten humanity. However, it is done in a way which explicitly disavows faith in any particular metaphysics, including the metaphysical presumption I have focused on: faith in the orderliness of scientific knowledge.

To pave the way for this pragmatic alternative to sceptical post-modernism I have outlined a philosophy that accepts the possibility of metaphysical disorder as a starting point. I have shown how a metaphysics constrained by empiricist concerns for the importance of experience can be developed which allows us to make sense of our plight as knowers who must make do in a world of uncertainty. We make do by learning to export knowledge, gained where we can get it, to other, very different situations, where worldly knowledge eludes us. My exemplar of a metaphysics of scientific practice for a disunified world has taken the form of an account of causal reasoning — an account which makes sense of the way causal attribution is practised by scientists, who, qua scientists, do not make metaphysical presumptions about the content of the world. This was complemented by an account of idealization, a way of thinking which allows us to export particular causal claims across contexts, and so apply highly general explanations to the world.

To prepare the way for acceptance of a metaphysics of disunity I went some way to excavating an underlying substratum of fundamentalism in the history of modern philosophy, and I argued against that funda-mentalism. I showed that there is an intimate relation between the history of modern philosophy and the threat perceived by modern philosophers in the possibility of disorder in the world. The philosophical position that I have arrived at is both epistemically and metaphysically pluralist. How-ever, the pluralism I advocate is one that, unlike many contemporary pluralisms, privileges scientific knowledge over its supposed alternatives.

Notes

1   The term 'special science' refers to any science other than physics.
2   The examples in this paragraph are from Nagel (1961, pp. 339-41).
3   See Causey (1977, especially chapters 4-7), Hooker (1981, especially part III), for detail of further debate about reduction and its role in uni-fication, and a demonstration of the complexity of those debates.
4   Kim (1992) argues along similar lines against earlier writers such as Hellman and Thompson (1975) who, following Fodor, reject reducibility on the grounds of multiple realisability.
5   I have argued for the compatibility of a weak notion of supervenience with the possibility of metaphysical disunity. If this combination turned out not to be viable, my inclination would be to abandon any commit-ment to supervenience. Dupré has argued against supervenience which he takes to be incompatible with metaphysical disunity (Dupré 1996a, 1996b).
6   The boat metaphor recurs in different contexts throughout Neurath's writings. This formulation is Neurath's '1932 Boat'. A discussion of the development of the boat metaphor is included in (Cartwright, Cat, Fleck and Uebel 1996).

7   In hindsight Neurath can be seen as ahead of his time in many ways. As Uebel puts it:

> Neurath anticipated the pursuit of historically informed theorising about science (associated with Kuhn); the denial of an "iron law" of scientific method (associated with Feyerabend); the naturalisation of epistemology (associated with Quine) (Uebel 1991, p. 6).

8   Reisch (1996) compares the actual development of the *International Encyclopedia of Unified Science* with Neurath's plans for it.

9   However, see Reisch (1997), who emphasises some of the differences between Dupré and Neurath.

10   Quoted in (Cat, Chang and Cartwright 1991, p. 106).

Bibliography

Armstrong, D.M. (1983), *What is a Law of Nature?*, Cambridge University Press: Cambridge.

Barnes, B. (1974), *Scientific Knowledge and Sociological Theory*, Routledge and Kegan Paul: London.

Berkeley, G. (1942), *A Treatise Concerning the Principles of Human Knowledge*, edited and annotated by T.E. Jessop, Nelson: London.

Bhaskar, R. (1975), *A Realist Theory of Science*, Leeds Book: Leeds.

Bigelow, J. and Pargetter, R. (1990), *Science and Necessity*, Cambridge University Press: Cambridge.

Bloor, D. (1976), *Knowledge and Social Imagery*, Routledge and Kegan Paul: London.

Bohman, J. (1991), *New Philosophy of Social Science: Problems of Indeterminacy*, the MIT Press: Cambridge.

Boyd, R. (1983), 'On the Current Status of Scientific Realism', *Erkenntnis*, 19, pp. 45-90.

Carnap, R. (1955), 'Logical Foundations of the Unity of Science' in O. Neurath, R. Carnap and C. Morris (eds.), *International Encyclopedia of Unified Science* Vol. 1, University of Chicago Press: Chicago, pp. 42-62.

Carroll, J. (1990), 'The Humean Tradition', *The Philosophical Review*, 99, pp. 185-219.

Carruthers, P. (1992), *Human Knowledge and Human Nature*, Oxford University Press: New York.

Cartwright, N. (1983), *How the Laws of Physics Lie*, Oxford University Press: New York.

Cartwright, N. (1989), *Nature's Capacities and Their Measurement*, Oxford University Press: New York.

Cartwright, N. (1992), 'Aristotelian Natures and the Modern Experimental Method' in J. Earman (ed.), *Inference, Explanation, and Other Frustrations*, University of California Press: Berkeley, pp. 44-71.

Cartwright, N. (1993), 'Is Natural Science "Natural" Enough? A Reply to Phillip Allport', *Synthese*, 94, pp. 291-301.

Cartwright, N. (1994), 'Fundamentalism vs The Patchwork Model of Laws', *Proceedings of the Aristotelian Society*, 94, pp. 279-92.

Cartwright, N., Cat, J., Fleck, L., and Uebel, T.E. (1996), *Otto Neurath: Between Science and Politics*, Cambridge University Press: Cambridge.

Cat, J., Chang, H. and Cartwright, N. (1991), 'Otto Neurath: Unification as the Way to Socialism' in J. Mittelstrass (ed.), *Einheit der Wissenschaften*, Akademie der Wissenschaften zu Berlin: Berlin.

Causey, R.L. (1977), *The Unity of Science*, Reidel: Dordrecht.

Chalmers, A. (1987), 'Bhaskar, Cartwright and Realism in Physics', *Methodology and Science*, 20, pp. 77-96.

Chalmers, A. (1993), 'So the Laws of Physics Needn't Lie', *Australasian Journal of Philosophy*, 71, pp. 196-205.

Chalmers, A. (1996), 'Cartwright on Fundamental Laws: A Response to Clarke', *Australasian Journal of Philosophy*, 74, pp. 150-2.

Cheng, P.W. and Novick, L.R. (1992), 'Covariation in Natural Causal Induction', *Psychological Review*, 99, pp. 365-382.

Clarke, S. (1995), 'The Lies Remain the Same: A Reply to Chalmers', *Australasian Journal of Philosophy*, 73, pp. 152-5.

Clarke, S. (1997), 'Pluralism Unconstrained', *International Studies in the Philosophy of Science*, 11, pp. 143-6.

Clifford, J. (1988), *The Predicament of Culture*, Harvard University Press: Cambridge.

Davidson, D. (1970), 'Mental Events' in L. Foster and J. Swanson (eds.), *Experience and Theory*, Duckworth: London, pp. 79-101.

Dijksterhuis, E.J. (1986), *The Mechanization of the World Picture*, Princeton University Press: Princeton.

Duhem, P. (1954), *The Aim and Structure of Physical Theory*, translated by P.P. Wiener, Princeton University Press: Princeton.

Dupré, J. (1993), *The Disorder of Things*, Harvard University Press: Cambridge.

Dupré, J. (1996a), 'Metaphysical Disorder and Scientific Disunity' in P. Galison and D. Stump (eds.), *The Disunity of Science*, Stanford University Press: Stanford, pp. 101-17.

Dupré, J. (1996b), 'The Solution to the Problem of Free Will', *Philosophical Perspectives*, 10, pp. 385-402.

Earman, J. (ed.) (1992), *Inference, Explanation, and Other Frustrations*, University of California Press: Berkeley.

Earman, J. (1993), 'Carnap, Kuhn, and the Philosophy of Scientific Methodology' in P. Horwich (ed.), *World Changes: Thomas Kuhn and the Nature of Science*, the MIT Press: Cambridge, pp. 9-36.

Feyerabend, P. (1963), 'How to be a Good Empiricist — A Plea for Tolerance in Matters Epistemological' in B. Baumrin (ed.), *Philosophy of Science: The Delaware Seminar*, Vol. 2, Interscience: New York, pp. 3-39.

Feyerabend, P. (1965), 'Problems of Empiricism' in R.G. Colodny (ed.), *Beyond the Edge of Certainty: Essays in Contemporary Science and Philosophy*, Prentice Hall: Englewood Cliffs, pp. 145-260.

Feyerabend, P. (1975), *Against Method*, New Left Books: London.

Fodor, J. (1974), 'Special Sciences, or the Disunity of Science as a Working Hypothesis', *Synthese*, 28, pp. 77-115.

Forman, P. (1971), 'Weimar Culture, Causality and Quantum Theory, 1918-1927: Adaptation by German Physicists and Mathematicians to a Hostile Intellectual Environment' in R. McCormmach (ed.), *Historical Studies in the Physical Sciences*, Vol. 3, University of Pennsylvania Press: Philadelphia.

Friedman, M. (1992a), 'Philosophy and the Exact Sciences: Logical Positivism as a Case Study' in J. Earman (ed.), *Inference, Explanation, and Other Frustrations*, University of California Press: Berkeley, pp. 84-98.

Friedman, M. (1992b), *Kant and the Exact Sciences*, Harvard University Press: Cambridge.

Galilei, G. (1953), *Dialogue Concerning the Two Chief World Systems Ptolemaic and Copernican*, translated by S. Drake, University of California Press: Berkeley.

Garfinkel, H. (1967), *Studies in Ethnomethodology*, Prentice Hall: Englewood Cliffs.

Gasking, D. (1955), 'Causation and Recipes', *Mind*, 64, pp. 479-87.

Geertz, C. (1975), *The Interpretation of Cultures: Selected Essays*, Hutchison: London.

Goodman, N. (1978), *Ways of Worldmaking*, Hackett: Indianapolis.

Goodman, N. (1983), *Fact, Fiction and Forecast*, Fourth Edition, Harvard University Press: Cambridge.

Green, T.H. (1894), 'Introduction to Hume's Treatise' in *The Works of Thomas Hill Green*, 3rd Edition, Longmans: London.

Grünbaum, A. (1954), 'Science and Ideology', *The Scientific Monthly*, July Edition, pp. 13-19.

Haack, S. (1990), 'Recent Obituaries of Epistemology', *American Philosophical Quarterly*, 27, pp. 199-212.

Haavelmo, T. (1944), 'The Probability Approach in Econometrics', *Econometrica*, 12 (Supplement).

Hacking, I. (1983), *Representing and Intervening: Introductory Topics in the Philosophy of Natural Science*, Cambridge University Press: Cambridge.

Harding, S. (1986), *The Science Question in Feminism*, Cornell University Press: Ithaca.

Harré, R. and Madden, E.H. (1975), *Causal Powers*, Blackwell: Oxford.

Heider, F. (1958), *The Psychology of Interpersonal Relations*, Wiley: Oxford.

Hellman, G. and Thompson, F. (1975), 'Physicalism, Ontology, Determination, and Reduction', *Journal of Philosophy*, 72, pp. 551-64.

Hempel, C.G. (1965), *Aspects of Scientific Explanation and Other Essays in the Philosophy of Science*, The Free Press: New York.

Hempel, C. G. (1988), 'Provisoes: A Problem Concerning the Inferential Function of Scientific Theories', *Errkentnis*, 28, pp. 147-64.

Hempel, C.G. and Oppenheim, P. (1948), 'Studies in the Logic of Explanation', *Philosophy of Science*, 15, pp. 135-75.

Hilton, D.J. (1988), 'Logic and Causal Attribution' in D.J. Hilton (ed.), *Contemporary Science and Natural Explanation: Commonsense Conceptions of Causation*, Harvester Press: Brighton, pp. 33-65.

Hooker, C.A. (1981), 'Towards a General Theory of Reduction, Parts I-III', *Dialogue*, 20, pp. 38-59, 201-36, 496-529.

Horton, R (1993), *Patterns of Thought in Africa and the West: Essays on Magic Religion and Science*, Cambridge University Press: Cambridge.

Hume, D.A. (1947), *Dialogues Concerning Natural Religion*, edited by N. Kemp Smith, Second Edition, Thomas Nelson and Sons: London.

Hume, D.A. (1978), *A Treatise of Human Nature*, edited by L.A. Selby-Bigge, Second Edition, Clarendon Press: Oxford.

Hylton, P. (1990), *Russell, Idealism and the Emergence of Analytic Philosophy*, Oxford University Press: Oxford.

Jackson, F. (1977), 'A Causal Theory of Counterfactuals', *Australasian Journal of Philosophy*, Vol. 55, pp. 3-21.

Kant, I. (1929), *Critique of Pure Reason*, translated by N. Kemp Smith, Macmillan Press: London.

Kelley, H.H. (1973), 'The Processes of Causal Attribution', *American Psychologist*, 28, pp. 107-28.

Kim, J. (1991), 'Supervenience as a Philosophical Concept', *Metaphilosophy*, 21, pp. 1-27.

Kim, J. (1992), 'Multiple Realisation and the Metaphysics of Reduction', *Philosophy and Phenomenological Research*, 52, pp. 1-26.

Kincaid, H. (1990), 'Defending Laws in the Social Sciences', *Philosophy of the Social Sciences*, 20, No. 1, pp. 56-83.

Kitcher, P. (1986), 'Projecting the Order of Nature' in R. Butts (ed.), *Kant's Philosophy of Physical Science*, Reidel: Dordrecht, pp. 201-35.

Koyré, A. (1943), 'Galileo and Plato', *The Journal of the History of Ideas*, Vol. 4, pp. 400-28.

Krajewski, W. (1977), *Correspondence Principle and Growth of Science*, Reidel: Boston.

Kuhn, T.S. (1962), *The Structure of Scientific Revolutions*, The University of Chicago Press: Chicago.

Kuhn T.S. (1977), 'Mathematical versus Experimental Traditions in the Development of Physical Science' in T.S. Kuhn, *The Essential Tension: Selected Studies in Scientific Tradition and Change*, The University of Chicago Press: Chicago, pp. 31-65.

Lakatos, I. (1970), 'Falsification and the Methodology of Scientific Research Programmes' in I. Lakatos and A. Musgrave (eds.), *Criticism and the Growth of Knowledge*, Cambridge University Press: Cambridge, pp. 91-195.

Laymon, R. (1989),'Cartwright and the Lying Laws of Physics', *The Journal of Philosophy*, 86, pp. 353-72.

Lewis, D. (1973), *Counterfactuals*, Harvard University Press: Cambridge.

Lewis, D. (1986), *Philosophical Papers: Volume II*, Oxford University Press: New York.

Locke, J. (1959), *An Essay Concerning Human Understanding*, edited and annotated by A.C. Fraser, Dover Publications: New York.

Losee, J. (1993), *A Historical Introduction to the Philosophy of Science*, Third Edition, Oxford University Press: Oxford.

Lyotard, J-F. (1984), *The Postmodern Condition: A Report on Knowledge*, translated by G. Bennington and B. Massumi, University of Minnesota Press: Minneapolis.

Lyotard, J-F. (1993), *The Postmodern Explained: Correspondence, 1982-1985*, University of Minnesota Press: Minneapolis.

Marx, K. (1968a), *Capital, Vols, I-III,* Progress Publishers: Moscow.

Marx, K. (1968b), *Theories of Surplus Value, Vols. I-III,* Progress Publishers: Moscow.

McGowan, J. (1991), *Postmodernism and its Critics,* Cornell University Press: Ithaca.

McMullin, E. (1985), 'Galilean Idealization', *Studies in the History and Philosophy of Science,* 16, pp. 247-73.

Murphy, C. (1981), 'Critical Notice - Philosophy and the Mirror of Nature', *Australasian Journal of Philosophy,* 59, pp. 338-45.

Nagel, E. (1961), *The Structure of Science,* Routledge and Kegan Paul: London.

Neurath, O. (1920), *Der Kampf,* 13.

Neurath, O. (1932), 'Protocol Statements', reprinted in O. Neurath. (1983), *Philosophical Papers 1913-1946,* edited and translated by R.S. Cohen and M. Neurath, Reidel: Dordrecht, pp. 91-9.

Neurath, O. (1935), 'Pseudorationalism of Falsificationism', reprinted in O. Neurath (1983), *Philosophical Papers 1913-1946,* edited and translated by R.S. Cohen and M. Neurath, Reidel: Dordrecht, pp. 121-31.

Neurath, O. (1937), 'Unified Science and its Encyclopedia', reprinted in O. Neurath (1983), *Philosophical Papers 1913-1946,* edited and translated by R.S. Cohen and M. Neurath, Reidel: Dordrecht, pp. 172-82.

Neurath, O. (1946), 'The Orchestration of the Sciences by the Encyclo-pedism of Logical Empiricism', reprinted in O. Neurath (1983), *Philo-sophical Papers 1913-1946,* edited and translated by R.S. Cohen and M. Neurath, Reidel: Dordrecht, pp. 230-42.

Norris, C. (1990), *What's Wrong with Postmodernism?,* Johns Hopkins University Press: Baltimore.

Nowak, L. (1980), *The Structure of Idealization,* Reidel: Boston.

Nowak, L. (1989), 'Abstracts Are Not Our Constructs. The Mental Constructs Are Abstracts', *Poznan Studies in the Philosophy of the Sciences and the Humanities,* 16, pp. 193-206.

Nowak, L. (1992), 'On the Concept of Adequacy of Laws. An Idealizational Explication' in J. Brzezinski and L. Nowak (eds.), *Idealization 111,* Rodopi: Amsterdam, pp. 245-54.

Okrent, M. (1984), 'Hermeneutics, Transcendental Philosophy and Social Science', *Inquiry,* 27, pp. 23-50.

Oppenheim, P. and Putnam, H. (1958), 'Unity of Science as a Working Hypothesis' in H.M. Feigl, M. Scriven and G. Maxwell, *Minnesota Studies in the Philosophy of Science, Vol. II,* University of Minnesota Press: Minneapolis, pp. 3-36.

Passmore, J. A. (1957), *A Hundred Years of Philosophy*, Duckworth: London.

Philipse, H. (1994), 'Towards a Postmodern Conception of Metaphysics: On the Genealogy and Successor Disciplines of Modern Philosophy', *Metaphilosophy*, 25, pp. 1-44.

Popper, K. (1935), *Logik der Forschung*, Julius Springer: Vienna.

Price, H. (1992), 'Metaphysical Pluralism', *The Journal of Philosophy*, 89, pp. 387-409.

Putnam, H. (1981), *Reason, Truth and History*, Cambridge University Press: Cambridge.

Rabinow, P. and Sullivan, W. (eds.) (1979), *Interpretive Social Science: A Reader*, University of California Press: Berkeley.

Reid, T. (1970), *An Inquiry into the Human Mind*, edited by T. Duggan, Chicago University Press: Chicago.

Reisch, G.A. (1991), 'Did Kuhn Kill Logical Empiricism?', *Philosophy of Science*, 58, pp. 264-77.

Reisch, G.A. (1996), 'Terminology in Action: Neurath and the *International Encyclopedia of Unified Science*' in E. Nemeth and F. Stadler (eds.), *Encyclopedia and Utopia: The Life and Work of Otto Neurath*, Kluwer: Dordrecht, pp. 79-86.

Reisch, G.A. (1997), 'How Postmodern was Neurath's Idea of Unity of Science?', *Studies in the History and Philosophy of Science*, 28, pp. 439-51.

Rorty, R. (1980), *Philosophy and the Mirror of Nature*, Princeton University Press: Princeton.

Rorty, R. (1991), *Essays on Heidegger and Others, Philosophical Papers, Vol. 2*, Cambridge University Press: Cambridge.

Roth, P. A. (1987), *Meaning and Method in the Social Sciences: A Case for Methodological Pluralism*, Cornell University Press: Ithaca.

Rouse, J. (1987), *Knowledge and Power: Towards a Political Philosophy of Science*, Cornell University Press: Ithaca.

Ruby, J. E. (1986), 'The Origin of Scientific "Law"', *Journal of the History of Ideas*, 47, pp. 341-60.

Russell, B. (1959), *My Philosophical Development*, George Allen and Unwin: London.

Salmon, W.S. (1989), 'Four Decades of Scientific Explanation' in P. Kitcher and W. Salmon (eds.), *Scientific Explanation, Minnesota Studies in the Philosophy of Science, Vol. XIII*, University of Minnesota Press: Minneapolis, pp. 3-219.

Sankey, H. (1993), 'Kuhn's Changing Conception of Incommensurability', *British Journal for the Philosophy of Science*, 44, pp. 759-74.

Skyrms, B. (1980), *Causal Necessity*, Yale University Press: New Haven.

Strawson, G. (1989), *The Secret Connexion*, Oxford University Press: Oxford.

Taylor, C. (1979), 'Interpretation and the Sciences of Man' in P. Rabinow and W. Sullivan (eds.), *Interpretive Social Science: A Reader*, University of California Press: Berkeley, pp. 25-71.

Taylor, C. (1980), 'Understanding in Human Science', *Review of Metaphysics*, 34, pp. 25-38.

Taylor, C. (1990), 'Rorty in the Epistemological Tradition' in A. R. Malachowski (ed.), *Reading Rorty*, Blackwell: Oxford, pp. 257-75.

Tooley, M. (1987), *Causation: A Realist Approach*, Oxford University Press: New York.

Tufte, E. (1974), *Data Analysis for Politics and Policy*, Prentice Hall: Englewood Cliffs.

Uebel, T.E. (1991), 'Otto Neurath and the Neurath Reception: Puzzle and Promise' in T.E. Uebel (ed.), *Rediscovering the Forgotten Vienna Circle*, Kluwer: Dordrecht, pp. 3-22.

van Fraassen, B.C. (1989), *Laws and Symmetry*, Oxford University Press: Oxford.

von Wright, G.H. (1971), *Explanation and Understanding*, Routledge and Kegan Paul: London.

Wahl, J. (1925), *The Pluralist Philosophies of England and America*, translated by F. Rothwell, Open Court: London.

Woodward, J. (1993), 'Capacities and Invariance' in J. Earman, A. Janis, G. Massey, and N. Rescher (eds.), *Philosophical Problems of the Internal and External World: Essays Concerning the Philosophy of Adolph Grünbaum*, The University of Pittsburg Press: Pittsburg, pp. 283-327.

Woodward, J. (1995), 'Causation and Explanation in Econometrics' in D. Little (ed.), *The Reliability of Economic Models*, Kluwer: Dordrecht, pp. 9-61.

Woolgar, S. (1988), *Science: The Very Idea*, Tavistock: London.

Wright, J.P. (1983), *The Sceptical Realism of David Hume*, University of Minnesota Press: Minneapolis.

Index

DATE D